THE DUKE LONGITUDINAL STUDIES OF NORMAL AGING
1955–1980

Ewald W. Busse, M.D., is Associate Provost, Dean Emeritus, and J. P. Gibbons Professor of Psychiatry at Duke University Medical Center. He was Chairman of the Department of Psychiatry from 1953 to 1974 and the founding Director (1957–1970) of the Center for the Study of Aging, where he was the Principal Investigator for the Longitudinal Studies of Aging. Dr. Busse has served as President of the American Psychiatric Association, the American Geriatrics Society, the Gerontological Society of America, the Southern Council of Deans, and, in 1983, the International Association of Gerontology. A director of the American Board of Psychiatry and Neurology for eight years, Dr. Busse was also a member of the Institute of Medicine of the Academy of Sciences. He has received numerous research and professional awards including the Edward B. Allen Award (1967), the Strecker Award (1967), the Kleemeier Award (1968), the Menninger Award (1971), the Modern Medicine Award (1972), the Freeman Award (1978), the Thewlis Award (1979), the Brookdale Award (1982), and the Sandoz Award (1983). Dr. Busse earned his B.A. degree at Westminster College which also awarded him the Sc.D. degree in 1960. He received his M.D. from Washington University in St. Louis in 1942.

George L. Maddox, Ph.D., is Professor of Sociology and of Medical Sociology (Psychiatry) at Duke University. Associated with the Center for the Study of Aging and Human Development since 1960, he served as Center Director from 1972 to 1982. Currently, he is Chairman of the University Council on Aging and Human Development. Dr. Maddox was a Founding Member of the Advisory Council of the National Institute on Aging (1975) and has served as President of the Gerontological Society of America (1978), as Chairman of the Section on Aging, American Sociological Association (1984), and as Secretary of the 1985 International Association of Gerontology Congress. His most recent book, coauthored with colleagues in economics, is *Inflation and the Economic Well-being of the Elderly* (1984). With Dr. Busse, Dr. Maddox received the 1983 Sandoz Award for longitudinal multidisciplinary research in aging. He was graduated from Millsaps College (1949) from which he also received an honorary Doctorate in Science (1984). His Ph.D. in Sociology is from Michigan State University (1956).

THE DUKE LONGITUDINAL STUDIES OF NORMAL AGING 1955–1980

OVERVIEW OF
HISTORY, DESIGN, AND FINDINGS

Ewald W. Busse, M.D.   George L. Maddox, Ph.D.

WITH

C. Edward Buckley, III, M.D.   Erdman B. Palmore, Ph.D.
Peter C. Burger, M.D.   Dietolf Ramm, Ph.D.
Linda K. George, Ph.D.   Ilene C. Siegler, Ph.D.
Gail R. Marsh, Ph.D.   F. Stephen Vogel, M.D.
Robert D. Nebes, Ph.D.   H. Shan Wang, M.B.
John B. Nowlin, M.D.   Max A. Woodbury, Ph.D.

Duke University
Center for the Study of Aging and Human Development

Springer Publishing Company
New York

Springer Publishing Company, Inc.
536 Broadway
New York, New York 10012

86 87 88 89 / 5 4 3 2

Library of Congress Cataloging-in-Publication Data

Busse, Ewald W.
  The Duke longitudinal studies of normal aging, 1955–1980.
  Bibliography: p. 143 Includes index.
  1. Aging—Physiological aspects—Longitudinal studies. 2. Central nervous sys-
tem—Diseases—Age factors—Longitudinal studies. 3. Cognitive disorders—Age
factors—Longitudinal studies. I. Maddox, George L. II. Buckley, C. Edward.
III. Title.
QP86.B826 1986   155.67   85-14773
ISBN 0-8261-4150-1

Printed in the United States of America

Contents

4 The Aging Central Nervous System, Cognitive Functioning, and Behavior: Psychometric and Behavioral Findings

5 Experimental Evidence from Ancillary Studies on Cognitive Changes with Age and Their Psychophysiological Correlates

Preface

Over the quarter century since the Longitudinal Studies were begun, the Duke Center has developed a variety of research, training, and service programs. All of these programs owe a special debt to the Longitudinal Studies. These studies represented a fundamental commitment to two propositions which stress the importance of integrating research, training, and service in the field of aging. The first of these propositions is that in order to teach effectively about human aging and to translate scientific knowledge into useful action, one must know something. The second proposition is that effective understanding of issues posed by human aging is not reducible to any single discipline.

This volume is more than a summary of findings from the Duke Longitudinal Studies. It is a history of why and how the studies emerged and the historical and institutional context in which they developed. It is an account of practical issues of research administration, of multidisciplinary interaction, and of the development of scientific careers.

The multidisciplinary emphasis of the Longitudinal Studies reflected a conscious philosophy and deliberate policy of the research team that planned and implemented the Duke Longitudinal Studies of Aging. The diverse disciplinary backgrounds of investigators attracted to the studies produced an exciting intellectual environment that sustained scholarly interest, molded careers in aging, and continued to attract new investigators to the project for over two decades. A strong sense of loyalty to the Longitudinal Studies was generated that contributed significantly to ensuring that the enormous amounts of data—literally millions of observations—were developed in an orderly way, maintained in accessible form, and analyzed systematically.

Throughout the history of the Longitudinal Studies the investigators met regularly, usually weekly, in what came to be called the Monday Night Meetings. The meetings, which were similar to those begun at the University of Colorado, where Ewald Busse first began his research on aging, were occasions for intellectual exchange, for planning, for surveillance of adherence to the research objectives and protocols, and for dealing with the myriad administrative details that are involved in the translation of good ideas into useful intellectual products. Those who have had the responsibility of managing large, multidisciplinary, longitudinal research projects involving human subjects can appreciate our satisfaction that the Duke Longitudinal Studies were completed without complaint from research subjects about their experiences in the studies. They will also appreciate our satisfaction that, coincident with submitting the final project report to the National Institute on Aging, we were able to place in the public domain adequately documented data sets representing a quarter century of research.

Just as the Duke Longitudinal Studies must be placed in context, so must this volume. Experienced scholars know that multidisciplinary longitudinal research entails considerable risk for investigators. Systematic reporting of research that attempts to capture adequately the essence of complex developmental processes perceived from a variety of disciplinary perspectives is necessarily delayed until the project is completed. In the meantime, one must settle for articles that report observations of research in progress. A quarter of a century is a long time to wait. And when the time for summation arrives, the task of synthesizing and presenting findings is an enormous and inevitably lengthy process. So, in the meantime, the investigators associated with the Duke Longitudinal Studies have produced literally hundreds of journal articles, book chapters, and reports to professional meetings. A large number of journal publications reporting various aspects of the longitudinal studies have been collected conveniently in three edited books, *Normal Aging* (Volumes I, II, and

III). A first systematic overview of sociological findings has been published by our colleague Erdman Palmore, *Social Patterns of Normal Aging* (Durham, Duke University Press, 1981). And Ilene Siegler (1983) has provided a comprehensive introduction to psychological data from the studies.

This volume has a distinctive role in plans for reporting a quarter century of research. We intend for this volume to provide a brief history, an introduction to basic research design and analysis issues, a synopsis of findings, a guide to a broad range of publications from the studies, and a perspective on what we set out to do and how we implemented our objectives. Some readers will be interested primarily in substantive findings or perhaps, more narrowly, in substantive findings of special relevance for medicine, psychiatry, psychology, social psychology, or sociology. We have responded to these diverse interests by highlighting substantive findings succinctly and referencing already published materials for those who wish additional information on specific issues immediately. Findings in various substantive areas are placed in a standard format that reviews the background of scientific questions and the research methodology used in answering the questions posed.

Other readers will be interested in the organizational and administrative issues in longitudinal research; in broad methodological issues of research design, sampling, and data analysis strategies; in issues of data management; or in the relationship between the main longitudinal studies and ancillary studies designed to illuminate special problems of substance or method. This volume provides a brief introduction to this broad range of issues. Not everyone will be interested in problems of administering multidisciplinary longitudinal research; of data cleaning, storage, retrieval, and use of statistical consultation or computer time; of maintaining a panel of subjects over time; or of relating a particular research project to the broader objectives of a university-based gerontology center. We have tried to present a concise but comprehensive overview of the Duke Longitudinal Studies in a way that provides a convenient introduction from which readers can get an overview of the total research project as well as the issues to be developed in greater detail in subsequent publications.

Particular attention is called to a number of ancillary studies associated with the longitudinal studies. The need and opportunity for special studies was suggested during the course of the longitudinal studies, as, for example, in a series of psychophysiological experiments on central nervous system functioning reported in Chapter Five. Because the methodology of these studies is not covered in the general methodological discussion of the longitudinal studies, the procedures used in these special studies are reported in some detail. Other ancillary studies are also reported in the context of various chapters. For example, special projects on data analysis problems appear in Chapter Two; an experiment in cerebral blood flow and evidence from research autopsies appear in Chapter Three; and a special study of the personal experience of potentially stressful life events appears in Chapter Four. In each instance these ancillary studies were designed so as to minimize interference with the objectives of the longitudinal studies and to enhance the overall usefulness of these studies.

We express our appreciation not only to the colleagues who assisted specifically in the presentation of this volume but also to the large number of colleagues noted in the acknowledgments who made the Duke Longitudinal Studies possible.

E. W. Busse, M.D.
Principal Investigator

George L. Maddox, Ph.D.
Research Coordinator

Acknowledgments

The contributions of the following persons to the Duke Longitudinal Studies—as investigators, consultants, colleagues, and students—are acknowledged with appreciation:

Banks Anderson, Jr., M.D.

Kurt W. Back, Ph.D.

Robert H. Barnes, M.D.

Dan Blazer, M.D.

Jack Botwinick, Ph.D.

Linda B. Bourke

Linda M. Breytspraak, Ph.D.

Robert G. Brown, Ph.D.

C. Edward Buckley, III, M.D.

Ewald W. Busse, M.D.

William Cleveland, Ph.D.

Louis D. Cohen, Ph.D.

Sanford I. Cohen, M.D.

Stephen Cutler, Ph.D.

Glenn C. Davis, M.D.

F. C. Dorsey, M.D.

Elizabeth B. Douglass, M.A.

Robert Dovenmuehle, M.D.

Carl Eisdorfer, Ph.D., M.D.

C. William Erwin, M.D.

E. Harvey Estes, M.D.

Judith Fox, Ph.D.

K. Regina Frayser, Ph.D.

E. L. Friedman, Ph.D.

Margaret Gatz, Ph.D.

Linda K. George, Ph.D.

J. Graham, Jr., M.D.

Stephen W. Harkins, A.B.

C. E. Henry, Ph.D.

Dorothy K. Heyman, A.B.

Carol Hogue, Ph.D.

Jacquelyne Jackson, Ph.D.

Frances C. Jeffers, M.A.

Bonnie Jericho

E. J. Kelty, M.Ps.Sc.

R. W. Kleemeier, Ph.D.

William H. Knisely, Ph.D.

Martin Lakin, Ph.D.

Janet Lowry, Ph.D.

Clark Luikart, M.A.

George L. Maddox, Ph.D.   Stephen Schroeder, Ph.D.
Kenneth G. Manton, Ph.D.   Barry M. Shmavonian, Ph.D.
Gail R. Marsh, Ph.D.   Ilene C. Siegler, Ph.D.
W. Edward McGough, M.D.   Albert J. Silverman, M.D.
David Mechanic, Ph.D.   Deborah A. Sullivan
Joanna D. Morris   Richard Tessler, Ph.D.
E. Gustave Newman, Jr., M.D.   James Thompson, M.D.
Claude R. Nichols, M.D.   Larry W. Thompson, Ph.D.
John B. Nowlin, M.D.   John P. Tindall, M.D.
Walter D. Obrist, Ph.D.   Adriaan Verwoerdt, M.D.
Morris A. Okun, Ph.D.   H. Shan Wang, M.B.
Erdman B. Palmore, Ph.D.   Stephen Weiler, M.D.
Eric Pfeiffer, M.D.   Alan D. Whanger, M.D.
Pat Prinz, Ph.D.   Frances Wilkie, M.A.
Dietolf Ramm, Ph.D.   Rosemary Wilson, Ph.D.
John B. Reckless, M.D.   Stuart Wilson, Ph.D.
William Satterwhite, Jr., M.D.   Max A. Woodbury, Ph.D.

Various institutes of the National Institutes of Health supported the Duke Longitudinal Studies with program project and center grants. This support is gratefully acknowledged.

We thank Mrs. Betty Parker Ray for preparing the final manuscript.

David J. Madden, Ph.D., assisted in the writing of Chapter 5, and his contribution is acknowledged with appreciation. Dr. Madden was a postdoctoral fellow in the laboratory of Dr. Robert Nebes and was an investigator in some of the projects reported in Chapter 5. He is now a Senior Fellow at the Duke Center.

Contributors

C. Edward Buckley, III, M.D., received his medical degree from Duke University in 1954. Following a tour of duty in the Navy, he completed his postgraduate medical education at Duke Medical Center in 1961. Dr. Buckley is a Professor of Medicine and an Assistant Professor of Immunology at Duke, where he also is a Senior Fellow of the Duke Center for the Study of Aging. His areas of interest are human immunology and disease.

Peter C. Burger, M.D., is Associate Professor of Pathology and Chief of the Division of Neuropathology at Duke University. He has co-authored the text *Surgical Pathology of the Central Nervous System and Its Coverings*. Presently, Dr. Burger serves as the Coordinating Pathologist for the Brain Tumor Cooperative Group and Chairman of the Brain Pathology Review Committee of the Pediatric Oncology Group. He received his M.D. from Northwestern University in Chicago.

Linda K. George, Ph.D., is Associate Professor in the Departments of Psychiatry and Sociology at Duke University and also serves as Associate Director of the Duke University Center for the Study of Aging and Human Development. Dr. George received her Ph.D. in Sociology from Duke University in 1975. Her dissertation was based on the Duke Longitudinal Studies, and she has been an active longitudinal investigator since that time. Dr. George has been Social Sciences Editor for the *Journal of Gerontology* and a member of NIMH's peer review panel on Life Course Research. Her major research interests include the social psychology of adulthood and old age, social factors in the onset and course of psychiatric illness, and health services research. Dr. George is the author of numerous books and articles including *Role Transitions in Later Life* and, with coauthors, *Quality of Life in Older Persons, The Importance of Mental Health Services to General Health Care,* and *Antecedents and Consequences of Retirement*.

Gail R. Marsh, Ph.D., is a Senior Fellow at the Duke University Center for the Study of Aging and Human Development, where he is also an Associate Professor of Medical Psychology in the Department of Psychiatry and a Lecturer in the Department of Psychology. He received his Ph.D. in Psychology from the University of Iowa in 1968. Dr. Marsh is on the editorial board of the *Journal of Gerontology* and an Editor of *Neurobiology of Aging* in the field of the psychological sciences. His areas of interest are cognitive psychology and electrical activity of the brain during the processing of information, especially as they may be altered by aging.

Robert D. Nebes, Ph.D., received his doctorate in 1971 from the California Institute of Technology for work with Dr. Roger Sperry on hemispheric specialization in split-brain humans. Following a three-year postdoctoral fellowship, he joined the faculty at Duke University, where his research centered on the effects of normal aging on memory and attention. In 1980, Dr. Nebes joined the faculty of the University of Pittsburgh and is presently an Associate Professor in the Department of Psychiatry. Currently, Dr. Nebes is focusing his research efforts on investigating the effects of Alzheimer's disease on semantic memory and attention.

John B. Nowlin, M.D., received his medical degree from Duke University School of Medicine (1959) and pursued postgraduate training in internal medicine. He has a long-term affiliation with the Duke Center for the Study of Aging and Human Development, currently as a Senior Research Fellow. Dr. Nowlin was responsible for the collection and evaluation of medical information in both Duke Longitudinal Studies of Aging. Research interests include health–behavior interactions as found among older persons.

Erdman B. Palmore, Ph.D., is Professor of Sociology in the Duke Departments of Psychiatry and Sociology and Senior Fellow in the Center for the Study of Aging and Human Development. He received his Ph.D. at Columbia University, M.A. at the University of Chicago, and B.A. at Duke University. Dr. Palmore has edited three collections of articles based on the longitudinal studies published as *Normal Aging I, II, III*; he also has authored *Social Patterns in Normal Aging* and numerous other books and articles on adult development and aging. Dr. Palmore is a Fellow of the American Sociological Association and the Gerontological Society of America and is currently President of the Southern Gerontological Society.

Dietolf Ramm, Ph.D., is Associate Research Professor and Associate Chairman of Computer Science at Duke University. He received his Ph.D. in Physics from Duke University in 1969 and was affiliated with the Duke Center for the Study of Aging from 1969 through 1982. Dr. Ramm has coauthored numerous articles in the fields of physics, psychiatry, and gerontology, and on the application of computers to these areas. Currently, he is working in the areas of computer science education and the use of technology to enhance that process.

Ilene C. Siegler, Ph.D., Associate Professor of Medical Psychology, Department of Psychiatry at Duke University, is a developmental psychologist who has a special interest in the psychology of adult development and aging. She is a Senior Fellow at Duke's Center for the Study of Aging and Human Development and currently directs two of the Aging Center's Postdoctoral Research Training Programs. Dr. Siegler headed the Psychological Laboratory for the Duke Longitudinal Studies from 1974 to 1980. Her research interests include longitudinal methodology, studies of intellectual and personality development across the lifespan, and health behavior relationships. She is the author, coauthor, or editor of over fifty publications in aging. Dr. Siegler received her undergraduate degree from the University of Michigan (1968) and her M.A. (1972) and Ph.D. (1973) degrees in developmental psychology from Syracuse University. She was a postdoctoral research fellow at Duke in psychology of aging and joined the faculty there in 1974. Currently, Dr. Siegler is President of the Division of Adult Development and Aging (Division 20) of the American Psychological Association and is Chair of the Research, Education, and Practice Committee of the Gerontological Society of America. She is a Fellow of both organizations.

F. Stephen Vogel, M.D., is Professor of Pathology at Duke University, where he has recently retired as Chief of the Neuropathology Division. He has held the offices of President of the American Association of Neuropathologists and of the International Academy of Pathology, U.S.-Canadian Division. Dr. Vogel served as consultant to NASA and, in conjunction with Dr. Webb Haymaker, studied the effects of cosmic radiation upon the central nervous system.

H. Shan Wang, M.B., Professor of Psychiatry and Senior Fellow of the Center for the Study of Aging and Human Development at Duke University, has been active for the past twenty years as a research clinician and teacher on mental health and mental disorders in the elderly. He was one of the pioneers in the development of the non-invasive xenon inhalation method for the determination of regional cerebral blood flow and has been an active investigator in many projects, especially those concerning the relationship of changes in brain function and behavior associated with aging.

Max A. Woodbury, Ph.D., has been Professor of Biomathematics and Professor of Mathematics at Duke University Medical Center since 1966. Presently, he is also Professor of Computer Science. A Senior Fellow at the Duke Center for the Study of Aging and Human Development, he is also an affiliated faculty member at the Duke University Center for Demographic Studies. Dr. Woodbury has been a Fellow at the Institute for Advanced Study at Princeton as well as a member of the faculty of several universities. From 1952 to 1960, he served as a consultant to Univac and CBS for the election night forecasts. He served as founding President and later as Secretary and Council Member for the Biomedical Information Processing Organization. A fellow in the American Statistical Association, the Institute of Mathematical Statistics, and the American Association for the Advancement of Science, Dr. Woodbury also has been a Council Member of the Association for Computing Machinery and the Institute for Management Sciences.

List of Tables and Figures

1

Historical Context

BACKGROUND OF THE
LONGITUDINAL STUDIES

Awareness of older adults and problems associated with aging in our society increased dramatically in the 1950s. A small group of scientists and professionals who anticipated aging as an issue of national interest had created the multidisciplinary Gerontological Society dedicated to research and training in aging in 1945. Scientists in a number of universities began systematic studies of aging that broadened interest in the aged as a social problem into interest in aging as a scientific problem. By the end of the 1950s, a productive relationship between scientists and federal agencies had produced three handbooks summarizing a substantial body of research on the biomedical, behavioral, and social aspects of aging. A White House Conference on Aging in 1961 brought together scientific and lay communities in a productive exchange that focused attention on a broad range of issues posed by an aging population. By 1965, the Congress had enacted Medicare and the Older Americans Act. This momentum was continued by a White House Conference on Aging in 1971 and during the decade of the 1970s scientific interest in aging was intense. The Congress authorized a multidisciplinary National Institute on Aging in the National Institutes of Health and the National Institute of Mental Health created a special center for the study of mental health of older persons. There was an explosion of scientific publications about aging.

These developments over the period of three decades, it is worthwhile to remember, had modest beginnings. With the benefit of hindsight, it is easy to be critical of the research undertaken in preceding decades and to identify lack of theoretical and methodological sophistication. Research on aging three decades ago was confined largely to the institutionalized elderly that constituted only a small portion of older adults, although we know now that most adults live out their lives competently and satisfactorily in various communities. Moreover, earlier studies were characteristically deficient methodologically; specifically, available research methods had not been developed to study aging as a complex, multivariate, continuous process. Modern data analysis techniques for multivariate longitudinal analysis and computing technology were in their infancy.

How the Longitudinal Studies Began

In this context Duke University created in 1955 a University Council on Aging with the intention of assembling and coordinating the resources of the institution for systematic, comprehensive study of aging. The groundwork was laid for creating in 1957 a center designed to bring together research investigators representing the best current disciplinary theory and methodology for systematic study of aging. The initial longitudinal study was one early expression of a strategy for systematic, continuing research on aging that would focus and use to a maximum degree the resources of the university.

E. W. Busse, who was to become the first chairman of the University Council and the founding director of the Duke Center, had developed an interest in aging at the University of Colorado in 1949–1950 while investigating central nervous system functioning. In collaboration with a neurosurgeon and a neurologist, Dr. Busse noted what appeared to be distinctive age-related patterns of brain activity. Many elderly persons exhibited disturbance in brain activity (a temporal focus reflected in EEG tracings) that resembled the pattern observed in epileptic young adults. This observation led in 1951 to the submission of a research proposal to the National Institutes of Health entitled "The Effects of Aging Upon the Central Nervous System—A Physiological and Psychological Approach." The specific objectives proposed included the standardization of the normal electroencephalograms of persons 60 years of age and over and the evaluation of CNS functioning in normal older people in contrast to those exhibiting pathological change. Other investigators in the project included Robert H. Barnes, M.D., Albert J. Silverman, M.D., Lawrence M. Frost, M.D., Margaret B. Thaler, M.D., and Milton G. Shy, M.D. This group began a series of regular seminars to explore the implications of their research and began to report their findings in 1953. The first published findings appeared in 1954 in *The American Journal of Psychiatry* (10:12, 1954). When Dr. Busse became chairman of the Department of Psychiatry in 1955, he was accompanied in this move by two of his collaborators, Dr. Barnes and Dr. Silverman.

Interest in systematic research on the aging central nervous system at Colorado was transplanted at Duke and was to thrive. The creation of a University Council occurred in 1955 and by 1957 Duke was designated by the National Institutes of Health as one of five regional centers for the study of aging. Duke's center was the only one of these five centers to survive. Four distinctive ideas played a particularly important role in the survival and development of interest in aging at Duke. First, a multidisciplinary perspective was perceived to be both desirable and necessary. An appropriately comprehensive study of the aging central nervous system (CNS) could not, Duke scientists concluded, conceivably be reduced to the domain of any single academic discipline. Understanding CNS functioning would require an understanding of interaction of the brain with other organic systems. Further, organic functioning has behavioral outcomes which are affected by cognitive and social factors.

Second, distinguishing intrinsic (primary) processes of aging from extrinsic (secondary) processes is fundamentally important. The proper study of aging necessarily requires investigation of populations of older persons living in communities in order to assess the interaction of intrinsic and extrinsic factors.

Third, the study of aging as a process implies longitudinal observation of individuals as they experience and respond to the multiple potential internal and external sources of the changes that affect their development and their experiences of aging.

And, fourth, longitudinal, multidisciplinary research on aging makes extraordinary demands on research organizations and on scientists which must be taken into account. In retrospect, it is clear that the vitality of the Duke Longitudinal Studies of Aging was enhanced by a firm institutional commitment to the systematic study of aging. This institutional commitment was reinforced by the visible, sustained commitment of investigators to a common enterprise they believed to be important.

All of the contributors to this volume have been associated with the Duke Longitudinal Studies for more than a decade and most of them considerably longer. The interaction of investigators over the years was extensive and intense not only in the daily interaction required by the studies but also in special weekly meetings of investigators. These meetings, begun coincident with the initiation of the Longitudinal Studies, provided throughout two decades of research a regular opportunity for interdisciplinary exchange of information and for smooth functioning of a complex project.

Research Goals and Objectives

In 1955 when the Duke Longitudinal Studies began, a comprehensive, systematic theory of aging to guide research did not exist. Clear methodological guidelines for designing research appropriate for investigating developmental processes were not available; reliable, valid, and standardized measurement procedures appropriate for the investigation of human aging on either experimental or social survey research were in very short supply. And there was very limited previous experience on which to draw about how to organize, implement, and sustain the commitment of scientists to the multidisciplinary, longitudinal research which appeared to be required.

The broad goal of the Duke Longitudinal Studies was, therefore, to explore and illustrate the potential and limits of the contribution of multidisciplinary, longitudinal research to the scientific understanding of human aging. This goal translated into some specific objectives for the development of a theoretical perspective, methodology, and the organization of multidisciplinary, longitudinal research.

Theoretical Perspective

In the 1950s, there was not—as there is not now—a master theory of human aging, a single paradigm which organizes and directs scientific thought and research on aging. Investigators that were attracted to the Longitudinal Studies at Duke did tend to share a theoretical perspective. This perspective was characterized by an appreciation of the implications of conceptualizing aging as a process involving persons interacting with and responding to their environments. This interaction ensures that it is difficult but necessary to disentangle developmental change in the later years (primary aging that would inevitably exhibit universally even in an optimally benign environment) and change explained by the response of persons to their environments (secondary aging). The extraordinary differences in average life expectancy between societies and among sub-groups in a single society and historical changes in life expectancy between and within societies indicate that observed patterns of human survival cannot be convincingly explained by biological theory alone. The potential for survival is, on average, demonstrably greater than is achieved. Further, the observed variation in a society in the behavior of individuals of identical chronological age cannot be convincingly explained by biology alone. To be born in a less rather than more developed nation or to live in poverty, ignorance and social isolation changes enormously not only the chances of survival into the later years but also patterns of morbidity and the experience of being old.

The perceived diversity of older adults directed the attention of Duke investigators to the study of aging in a community context where the overwhelming majority of adults are found. The community was perceived as the context in which normal aging could be observed. The concept of *normal* aging was used initially to connote naturally developmental processes in later life as distinct from pathological processes which are more likely to be attributable to disease rather than aging. In retrospect, *normative* aging may have been a better choice and even this concept would have required a cautionary statement; caution is required because observed patterns of primary and secondary aging processes of particular cohorts of older persons in a longitudinal study may be time-bound and culture-specific. In the past decade, social scientific research has documented changes in the size and socioeconomic composition of different cohorts (i.e., persons born about the same time) of older people reflecting different experiences as they interact with changing environments over the course of their lives. Different historical experiences of particular cohorts produce potentially different individual biographies which would require qualification of any generalization a scientist might make about the normalcy or normativeness of observed patterns of developmental change.

Scientific theory has multiple uses. The most elemental use is to describe accurately and as completely as possible observed regularities in complex events. An associated use is to enhance intellectual appreciation of the range of interacting variables which appear to be important in the understanding of aging processes. At this level, theory is essentially a set of empirical descriptions and generalizations. At a more sophisticated level, theory becomes paradigms of related propositions which permits events and processes to be predicted and, ultimately, controlled. The prototype of sophisticated theory is found in experimental research.

In the 1950s in the absence of an established comprehensive theoretical paradigm for the study of normative aspects of primary aging processes, the first Duke Longitudinal Study set as its initial goal the identification of empirical descriptions and generalizations about the experience of aging in a community setting. Particular attention was given to identification and interaction of a broad range of individual and social variables suggested by published research to be potential determinants of aging processes. The proposed use of longitudinal research design was intended to permit description of intra-individual change over time and inter-individual differences and differential patterns of change. With a broad range of biomedical, behavioral, and social variables measured within a defined study population, the population was viewed as participating in a natural, quasi-experiment and, as such, multiple observations of the same individuals could be the basis of testing the power of particular variables or types of variables to explain and predict, with appropriate caution, observed individual changes and differential inter-individual change.

The primary initial interest in systematic description of aging processes was complemented in two ways. In 1967 the scientific investigators of the initial longitudinal study proposed a second study. Additional details about this second study which was begun in 1968 will be provided in the next section of this chapter and in Chapter Two. It is sufficient here to comment on the implications of the additional longitudinal study for development of theory. A decade of experience in the initial Duke study established the significance of the range of variables used to study aging processes but, more importantly, confirmed the significance of the dynamic interaction of these variables over time. Interest in the explanation and prediction of aging processes for individuals and of inter-individual differential in these processes was heightened. Further, in the mid-1960s what came to be called "the age/period/cohort problem" (APC) emerged. The second Duke Study, initiated in 1968, focused on the dynamic interaction of variables in processes of aging and took into consideration the methodological implications of the APC problem (see, e.g., Maddox and Wiley, 1976; and Maddox and Campbell, 1985).

The heart of the APC problem is the recognition that in research on aging processes, chronological age, the time of measurement (i.e., the exogenous environmental variables impinging on individuals) and location in a cohort (i.e., individuals with potentially different historical experience related to the environments in which they were born and reared) are typically confounded. Duke investigators understood the issue. Their theoretical perspective for the study of aging individuals in the context of environment anticipated the problem posed for disentangling primary and secondary aging processes. Further, they appreciated the limitation of studying longitudinally a limited range of subjects who represented a limited range of cohorts.

With these considerations in mind, the investigators proposed a second study with two distinctive characteristics. The new study was intended to focus on adaptation to major life events using the theoretical perspective of stress theory. This perspective suggests that common age-related events such as retirement, illness, widowhood, and the departure of the last child challenge individuals to adapt and that they respond and adapt differentially. Events in themselves are potentially but not inherently stressful in a universal way. Adaptation is determined substantially by the availability and use of existing physiological, psychological, and social resources. Further, the second study was designed methodologically to cover a period of six years so that persons in a number of five-year age cohorts would move from one age category to the next.

A second complementary strategy in the Duke studies of normal aging involved a number of ancillary studies. These special studies— on psychophysiological aspects of cognition, cerebral lateralization,

cerebral blood flow, the personal experience of life events, special
statistical problems in longitudinal data analysis and brain morphology at autopsy—were designed to pursue in depth selected basic
issues raised in the longitudinal studies which could not be incorporated early into these studies without disrupting them. The first four
of the studies concentrated on issues in CNS functioning, were experimental and designed to test specific hypotheses. The fifth study
explored the personal meaning of life events to those who had experienced them. The sixth study explored ways to solve topics of particular importance in longitudinal studies—missing data and data
analytic procedures designed to explicate the complex interaction of
variables in aging processes. The autopsy study had two purposes.

The autopsy study explored the feasibility of bringing to autopsy
identified subjects in the first longitudinal study for whom observations over a period of two decades on biological, psychological, and
social performance were known. The opportunity to relate observed
patterns of functioning with brain structure at death was also important in assessing hypotheses about relationships between CNS structure and function.

The development and uses of a theoretical perspective in the
Duke Longitudinal Studies are illustrated in the chapters which follow. For the most part, the perspective has identifiable disciplinary
origins and is used to address disciplinary questions in the biomedical, behavioral, and social aspects of aging processes. The emphasis
is variously on the description of regularity in observed patterns of
aging (the first longitudinal study) and the testing of disciplinary and
occasionally interdisciplinary hypotheses in the second longitudinal
study and in the experiments of the ancillary studies.

Methodology

A theoretical perspective necessarily has implications for the design
of research. A second objective of the Duke Longitudinal Study,
therefore, was to design research appropriate for the study of aging
processes in which biomedical, behavioral, and social factors interact
over time in natural settings. The details of sampling procedures for
the two longitudinal studies are reported in Chapter Two and will
not be repeated here.

The representativeness of study populations is a critical issue if one is to generalize findings. In multidisciplinary, longitudinal research, the recruitment and retention of subjects presents a difficult problem, particularly when subjects are required to give several days regularly (three days for the first longitudinal and one for each observation). Initial refusal to participate in the Duke studies and subsequent drop-out (refusal, migration, death) present complicated problems for the analysis and generalization of data. The Duke Longitudinal Studies did not provide ideal solutions for these problems but did succeed in identifying and explicating problems in useful ways in the analysis and generalization of data. Reports of findings illustrate carefully detailed and cautious uses of data that do not exceed their identified limitations.

The different scientific objectives of the two longitudinal studies and of the ancillary experimental studies have already been noted. The design of the second longitudinal study to incorporate what was at the time a new interest in cohort differences was innovative. In retrospect, given what is now known about the complexities of adequately designed cohort-sequential research, the Duke innovation appears to be modest. It did not seem so modest at the time and the innovation did explicate both the potential and limitations of wedding longitudinal and cohort-sequential research designs.

Conceptualization, operationalization, and measurement of variables in longitudinal research which reflect the state-of-the-art initially almost inevitably tend, in retrospect, to be dated and less adequate than current alternatives. The simple fact is that insuring continuities in and comparability of repeated measurement in longitudinal research—which is its strength—exacts a price. This fact does not require an apology. Rather it requires a clear recognition of the problem and adequately detailed reporting of the decisions made and why they were made at the time. Publications of the Duke Longitudinal Studies meet this requirement.

Developments in computation and statistical analysis over the past decade and a half have been extraordinary. When the longitudinal studies began, its investigators had been trained, if they were trained at all, to punch computer cards by hand and to use counter-sorter machines. And even though computing hardware was fairly sophisticated in the 1960s, the kinds of software required to make large-scale data analysis convenient simply did not exist. It is notable that in the late 1950s and 1960s special software—Tape Storage and Retrieval (TSAR)—was designed at Duke specifically for the Longitudinal Studies. TSAR packaged all the conventional statistical analysis procedures of the day conveniently and in ways that could be and were learned and used by scientific investigators working on the longitudinal studies.

The solution of problems in the management of missing data and in the analysis of longitudinal observations, which are critical in the kind of research in aging undertaken at Duke, is now understood by and available to every well-trained beginning graduate student today. This was not the case in 1955 or for a long time thereafter. As will be noted in greater detail in Chapter Two, Duke investigators explicated and provided some useful solutions to some basic problems in analysis of longitudinal data. The solution of the "missing data problem," the assessment of the power of different multivariate analysis techniques, and a workable solution of the APC problem made it possible for the Duke Studies to have the benefit of the state-of-the-art in longitudinal data analysis.

Developing a Multidisciplinary Research Team

The third objective of the Duke Longitudinal Studies, while practical and organizational in its focus, was perceived to be a necessary condition of achieving the objectives of developing theory and its related methodology. This objective was the creation and maintenance of the multidisciplinary investigators who would commit a significant portion of their scientific careers to a complex project that would certainly cover many years. The required commitment was achieved to an unusual degree. The investigators who contributed to this volume all remain at Duke; most of them were involved in the longitudinal studies for more than a decade.

Two observations from experience help explain the observed stability of career commitment. The first observation stresses the recognition that individual investigators in multidisciplinary research must be able to relate their participation to disciplinary career goals. The second notes that participation in multidisciplinary research is not equally congenial to all scientists. Only experience in longitudinal, multidisciplinary research reveals whether a scientific investigator can tolerate and thrive intellectually in this type of research environment.

As a matter of principle and policy, longitudinal research team investigators at Duke were expected and encouraged to maintain an identification with their primary discipline. At the same time, these investigators were provided multiple and regular opportunities (1) to explore the potential advantages of working cooperatively on a single research population in which evidence generated by colleagues in other disciplines would be available; (2) to share common research support services (space, technicians, computation, statistical consultation) that would not likely be available to any single investigator; and (3) to interact formally and informally with research team colleagues continually with an intensity of their own choosing.

Experience and training lead some investigators to tolerate and accept, and occasionally to prefer and benefit from, multidisciplinary team research. Individual investigators initially attracted to the Longitudinal Studies were provided a great deal of latitude to explore their preferences and to maintain identification with the longitudinal studies team only if they found that experience stimulating and productive. A cohesive research team did emerge from those initially attracted throughout the studies. Regular weekly meetings of the research team provided a major opportunity to test the tolerance and preferences of investigators for longitudinal research. Perceived pressure for immediately publishable material winnowed out some investigators. Others found that their scientific training had produced a preference for disciplinary, focused, experimental inquiry that was in basic conflict with the requirements of multidisciplinary, longitudinal research.

ADMINISTRATIVE ISSUES

Maintaining Records

The necessity of recording decisions made by the longitudinal research team about the conduct of their joint inquiry was recognized from the beginning. Records constitute the historic memory of a group regarding why a particular theoretical or methodological perspective was used in the development of a research design or measurement technique and both why and how, as experience required, modifications in design and technique could be accommodated. In this sense, the history of the Duke Longitudinal Studies is recorded in an exemplary fashion. This is reflected in the capability, after a quarter century, to produce from records of the weekly seminars documentation of the completed data sets from both longitudinal studies. Further, the complete protocols of all information on all longitudinal subjects are preserved on microfiche. Such careful documentation permits the project to place adequately documented Duke longitudinal data sets in the Duke Center's Survey Data Laboratory and Data Archive for use by themselves, by other research investigators, and by students and research fellows in training.

Quality Control in Longitudinal Research

Responsibility for the selection and modification of measurement procedures, administration of these procedures, and documentation of results was assigned to individual investigators or groups of investigators whose disciplinary expertise was most relevant for specific variables included in the longitudinal studies. Access to all variables by all longitudinal investigators was assured. However, as a matter of policy, a longitudinal investigator including a variable outside his or her disciplinary expertise in reports intended for publication was obligated to discuss the matter with appropriate colleagues in whose domain the variable fell. Typically, draft reports were presented to the entire longitudinal research team prior to publication. Investigators not identified as members of the longitudinal team who requested access to the data were required to submit research protocols for approval by the team prior to accessing the longitudinal project data and to present draft reports of findings to the team for review prior to publication.

Public Use of Duke Longitudinal Study Data

Although science is a public enterprise that requires the publication and public review of procedures and findings, scientific data sets are by convention and by law typically the possession of the investigators who generate the data. Some data sets, particularly those generated by federal agencies, are designed for public use, but this is not usually the case for data sets generated by individual scientists even when they are supported by public funds.

The research team of the Duke Longitudinal Studies decided that simultaneously with the submission of its final report to the National Institute on Aging at the completion of the studies, the data sets and related documentation and subject files (subjects are not identified by name in the files, assuring adequate protection of rights) would be placed in the public domain. This decision reflected several factors. Members of the research team who had benefitted from interaction with colleagues were confident they would continue to benefit from interaction with additional investigators who would be attracted. Further, they were acutely aware that large-scale, expensive data sets have earned the reputation of being seriously under-utilized. Maximizing the use of the data made sense. Finally, the research team members were aware that constant interaction breeds familiarity and similarity in the theoretical and methodological perspectives of investigators. The possibility of attracting and interacting with other investigators with different perspectives was intellectually appealing.

The longitudinal data sets have proved to be particularly attractive to and widely used by graduate students and post-doctoral fellows at Duke and elsewhere and increasingly by experienced investigators who have not had previous association with the Duke Longitudinal Studies. The full potential of these studies, in a sense, remains to be realized and may be realized more fully as the availability and easy access to the data sets becomes known. The Second Longitudinal Study data set is adequately documented and is currently available. The First Study is also available but convenient access is complicated by the size of a data set which includes eleven rounds of observations covering thousands of variables and volumes of documentation. A project to simplify access to the First Study data set is currently in process.

2

Methodology: The Strategy of Research Design and Inquiry

Measuring changes with age in the same individuals over time in order to compensate for the well-known weaknesses of cross-sectional studies was a key issue in the Duke Studies. Cross-sectional studies that document differences in the characteristics or behavior of different ages at a single point in time invite the inference that the differences reflect changes attributable to aging. Recognition of this problem was an important step in the decision to study aging processes as distinct from documenting differences among persons whose age also places them in different age cohorts. The problem can be illustrated simply. Assume that in a cross-sectional study in 1980 an investigator found differences in indices of health status or intellectual performance or attitudes toward retirement between 60 and 70 year olds. If the observed differences are attributable to aging, then the 70 year olds provide an estimate of the characteristics of the 60 year olds when they become 70. Similarly, the 60 year olds describe accurately the characteristics of current 50 year olds a decade later and the characteristics of 70 year olds ten years earlier. These are highly suspect assumptions which have been increasingly discredited by research. It is this issue of distinguishing age-differences and age-changes which underlies contemporary interest in age/period/cohort analysis.

Longitudinal studies have other advantages. Antecedents can be distinguished from consequences in processes of change. Consistent trends in patterns of change can be distinguished from temporary fluctuations. Retrospective distortion of information about past events is minimized. Early warning signs of disease or death can be studied and predictors of longevity or other outcomes can be studied prospectively. The dynamic interactive effects of change in biomedical, behavioral, and social variables can be assessed.

Longitudinal studies of limited samples (the initial Duke Longitudinal Study is an example) do risk confounding changes related to aging with changes related to the response of different cohorts to changing historical environments. This risk was taken into account and reduced by designing the second Duke Longitudinal Study to permit assessment of possible cohort effects. Other potential limitations of longitudinal studies—high cost, a long time commitment, the practical difficulties of sample maintenance—should be noted. In balance, however, the advantages of longitudinal design have, in the view of the Duke longitudinal research team, outweighed the disadvantages.

Multidisciplinary longitudinal research requires the integration, not just the juxtapositioning, of different theoretical and methodological perspectives in designing studies that promise to serve both individual and collective purposes in both the short and long run. The team of investigators that planned and implemented the Duke studies, for example, has included internists, immunologists, ophthalmologists, radiologists, dermatologists, psychiatrists, psychologists, sociologists, social workers, and statisticians. The essential characteristics of the longitudinal studies they designed and implemented can be described briefly.

TWO LONGITUDINAL STUDIES

Objectives

The First Study

Officially designated as a study of ''the effect of aging upon the central nervous system: a physiological, psychological, and sociological study of aging,'' the first longitudinal was planned and implemented in 1955. Preliminary investigation and pilot studies were initiated to determine whether a longitudinal study of community residents was feasible, practical, and of scientific value. In their initial studies of aging and brain function, E. W. Busse and his colleagues in Colorado had already noted that most of the studies of the aging processes had been carried out utilizing subjects who were patients—they were institutionalized, receiving medical services, and/or assistance from social agencies. A community study of older persons in normal settings was proposed to provide a more balanced perspective.

The initial plan was to investigate the processes of aging among a panel of noninstitutionalized males and females, 60 years of age and over, from the time of initial observation to death. One indication that the practical implications of studying panelists until all had died were not fully understood, is that there were 58 of the initial 270 participants in the first study panel still living when the Duke investigators decided to end data collection twenty-one years later in 1976. In 1981 there were still 26 panelists known to be living. Systematic data collection was officially terminated because, with an increasing number of subjects having to be studied at home, scientific return became too low to justify the high economic cost. As has been and will be noted again, a special autopsy study was initiated in 1980 with 10 surviving panelists from the first study.

The First Longitudinal Study was intended to be exploratory. Its organization was intended to facilitate the accumulation of the widest possible range of observations on elderly subjects residing in the community by investigators with a variety of theoretical and methodological perspectives. And, as already noted, the study was not guided by any single theory of aging. The focus was on hypothesis generation and testing by investigators who brought different but complementary theoretical perspectives to bear on analysis of the data from a single panel of subjects.

The first study, therefore, offered each investigator of the research team an opportunity for contact with colleagues with different theoretical interests and perspectives and an opportunity for the use of the data of other investigators as control variables in their own research undertakings. Because of its twenty-one year span, the First Longitudinal Study was uniquely suited for the analysis of predictors of longevity and of factors related to maintenance of biological, behavioral, and social functioning.

The Second Study

As the First Longitudinal Study progressed, it became apparent to the research team that, in order to understand the continuities as well as the variations in the aging processes fully and to take the influence of changing environments into account, a new study was desirable. A Second Longitudinal Study was planned in the mid-1960s by the research team and was implemented in 1968 to complement the first study in three specific ways:

1. The new study included some *younger* adults (46–70), that is those often referred to as "late middle age."
2. Its focus was on patterns of *adaptation* to the probable stresses of the middle and late middle years such as illness episodes, widowhood, retirement, and changes in living arrangements.
3. It was designed to allow *cross-sequential* analysis in order to partial out the effects of aging from differences between cohorts and influenced by time of measurement.

Thus, the second study shared with the first study an interest in normal processes of physical, psychological, and social aging observed in a panel of community residents, but was distinguished by its emphasis on *adaptation* to normal stresses of *middle* and later life and by its *cross-sequential* design.

Sampling Strategy and Samples

The First Study

A panel of noninstitutionalized persons aged 60 to 94 was implemented in 1955. Over the next 21 years, eleven observations of surviving panelists were completed. Relatively complete information is available initially on 270 persons, 260 of whom were in the first round of observations; 10 subjects were added in the second round and initial data for this addition were coded as though they were in the first round of observations. Panel survivors were examined periodically, and the time between examinations decreased as the research progressed. For example, approximately 36 months separated the first and second examinations and approximately 12 months separated examinations in rounds 10 and 11. The 11th and final examination of 44 persons was made in 1976 (Table 2.1). Table 2.1 shows the number of persons in each round with relatively complete data from physical, psychological, and social examinations. The total number of participants in any round is greater than the number with data from any one type of examination because some participants missed some of the examinations. This fact, commonly observed in longitudinal studies of community subjects, produces the "missing data problem." Initially, the mean age of subjects was 70.8 years; at the last observation, the mean age was 85.2 years; 52 percent were female and 63.8 percent were white.

The panelists, who were recruited to participate in periodic, intensive, two-day examinations, were selected from a pool of volunteers in Durham, Orange, and Wake Counties, North Carolina. Selection procedures insured that age, sex, racial, and socio-economic characteristics of panelists would reflect the known range and distribution of these characteristics in the community. Essential control variables were therefore available for hypothesis testing (Palmore, 1970; Maddox, 1962, reprinted in Palmore, 1970).

Table 2.1. Participants in the First Longitudinal Study by Round

Round #	Dates	Total # of Participants**	Number with: Physicals	Number with: Psychological	Number with: Social Data
1	3/55–5/61*	270	268	267	268
2	9/59–5/61	183	181	182	182
3	1/64–3/65	178	138	140	172
4	10/66–6/67	138	109	110	136
5	6/68–1/69	110	92	93	107
6	2/70–8/70	108	94	92	101
7	1/72–5/72	81	65	60	74
8	2/73–8/73	68	62	57	54
9	4/74–9/74	57	55	52	55
10	12/74–8/75	56	53	47	51
11	3/76–8/76	44	42	41	41

*Ten of the participants in the first round had their first examinations after the second round of examinations had started for other participants.
**The total number of participants is larger than the number with any one type of examination because some participants missed some of the examinations.

The panel of subjects in the first study is adequate for testing a wide range of hypotheses interrelating different biomedical, behavioral, and social variables and characterizing changes in variables over time in the later years of life. The panel data, however, are not adequate for generalizations about the distribution of characteristics or variables among older persons generally. Panelists at the first examination tended to be of higher social status, in better health, and more active than older persons generally. This difference is commonly observed in all longitudinal studies of older persons and even in social surveys of older persons employing probability sampling procedures, because advantaged persons tend to be more likely than others to participate in such research studies (Maddox, 1962) and to survive. For further detailed information on the panelist in the First Longitudinal Study see *Normal Aging I* (Palmore, 1970).

The Second Study

The second panel, instituted in 1968, included an age-sex stratified random sample of 502 persons aged 45–69 at the time of sampling. Panelists were drawn randomly primarily from the membership list of the major health insurance association in the area. This list included the majority of the middle and upper income residents of Durham County, North Carolina, under age 65; the list included some working class residents of the county covered by industrial group policies but the completeness of the coverage cannot be estimated.

Few persons over age 65 belonged to the association, since medicare coverage was provided separately. Therefore, the panel was supplemented by a sub-sample of 32 persons aged 65–69 from the record files of Duke Medical Center. This sub-sample proved to be somewhat above the average in socio-economic status.

Illiterate persons were excluded from the study because they could not take the necessary written tests. Institutionalized or homebound persons were excluded because they could not come for the full range of examinations. Blacks were not included in the second study because their inclusion in a relatively small total sample would have made adequate statistical analysis by race impossible. It should be noted that Blacks were included in the panel of the first study.

Within each of ten age-sex categories, names were randomly drawn from lists provided by the health organization and medical center and contacted for examinations until quotas in each category were filled. The quotas were designed to insure at least 44 persons for retesting in each of the cohorts at the end of six years, assuming a 10 percent dropout rate and the age-sex specific mortality rates. Because the study required eight hours of examinations without compensation, about half of the persons contacted initially refused to participate.

Table 2.2 summarizes panel participation by round over the course of the second study and the number for whom relatively complete data of different types are available.

Adequacy of Initial Sample of the Second Study

In order to estimate how the final sample might differ from the other members of the health association and medical center, the research team compared the study sample with a sample of those who refused to participate, using information from a telephone survey of nonparticipants. This comparison showed that the participants were quite similar to the nonparticipants on education, marital status, and health rating (Table 2.3). The panel participants were different from nonparticipants in that 14 percent more of the panelists reported they had a private physician; but this could have been caused by the fact that the participants were encouraged to report the name of a "private physician" to whom a report of the medical examination could be sent.

Table 2.2. Participants in the Second Longitudinal Study by Round

Round #	Dates	Total # of Participants*	Physicals	Psychological	Social Data
				Number with:	
1	8/68–4/70	502	502	502	502
2	8/70–3/72	443	438	438	443
3	6/72–7/74	386	384	383	383
4	8/74–10/76	375	274	275	275

*The total number of participants in each round may be larger than the number with any type of examination because some participants missed some of the examinations.

Table 2.3. Characteristics of Participants, Second Study, Compared to Nonparticipants

Characteristic	Participants (N=502)	Non participants (N=94)
Median years of school completed	12.5	12.3
Percent married	85%	85%
Mean health rating (4 point scale)	2.2	2.1
Percent with private physician	90%	76%

In order to estimate how the initial sample of the second study might differ from the U.S. population, the research team compared panelists with all white persons in the U.S. aged 45–69 (using 1970 Census statistics). The panelists were somewhat more likely to be married, employed, better educated, and in the upper level occupations (Table 2.4).

Table 2.4. Characteristics of the Study Sample, Second Study, Compared to U.S. White Persons Aged 45–69

Characteristic	Sample Study	U.S. White 45–69
Percent married	85%	79%
Percent employed	66%	59%
Median years of school completed	12.5	11.1
Percent professional or managers	35%	25%

These comparisons indicate that panelists of the second study were, on balance, fairly similar to the characteristics of others in the populations from which they were drawn. But panelists tended to be somewhat above average for all white Americans in the designated age range. Therefore, any generalizations from this study to older adults should be made with these differences in mind.

Survivors of the original sample of the Second Longitudinal Study were reexamined every two years until the fourth and final round in 1974–76. At this time, there were 375 survivors.

Sample Attrition

Characteristics of *dropouts* from both studies have been documented in considerable detail. Coding procedures which identify not only the time of dropout but also the reasons for doing so facilitate analysis of this important issue in longitudinal research. Analysis and reporting of longitudinal data must be done with the potential effect of dropout in mind.

The First Study

Participation and attrition patterns varied greatly between the two studies. Special efforts were made to retain as many of the panelists as possible, including the use of home visits which were instituted at the 5th examination of the first study. Contact with subjects who had moved from the Durham area was maintained whenever possible. Sometimes, e.g., arrangements could be made for study participants who had moved away to be tested when they came back to Durham for a visit.

The major form of attrition in the first study was from death, with 16 percent dead by Round 1 and 79 percent by Round 11. The importance of assessing the effect of dropout can be illustrated by the association between measured intelligence and continued participation in the panels. Both attrition and mortality have been shown to be significantly related to lower cognitive performance for both intelligence (Botwinick and Siegler, 1980) and memory (Siegler, McCarty & Logue, 1982).

The Second Study

The major attrition in this study was due to refusal to continue (15%) rather than death (10%). As the panelists in the second study were middle aged, competing personal commitments and scheduling difficulties were greater than for panelists in the first study; but other factors were involved. For example, analyses of the personality predictors of dropout in the second study (Rusin & Siegler, 1975) found that dropout was predicted by anxiety. Dropout was also predicted by poorer health (Siegler & Nowlin, 1979).

Variables and Indices

About a thousand variables and indices were coded for each participant in the initial and subsequent round of both longitudinal studies. Major types of these variables and indices are presented in Tables 2.5 (the first study) and 2.6 (the second study). The broad range of

Table 2.5.   Types of Variables and Indices in the First Longitudinal Study

Medical history (original and interim)	Laboratory studies
	Urinalysis
Physical examination	Blood morphology
Neurological examination	Blood chemistry
Mental status	Serologic test for
Depression and	syphillis
hypochondriasis	Cholesterol
Dermatological examination	Urea nitrogen
Ophthalmological examination	Immunology
Visual fields	Medical data
Acuity	Psychological data
Color perception	Rorschach
Depth perception	Aspiration level
Color photographs	Wechsler Adult
Audiometry	Intelligence Scale
Pure tone	Reaction time
Speech threshold	Social history and
Electroencephalogram	information
Electrocardiograph	Retirement data
Chest x-ray	Activities
	Attitudes
	Longevity

Table 2.6. Types of Variables and Indices in the Second Longitudinal Study

Independent Variables (Indexing resources mediating adaptation)	Dependent Variables (measures of adaptation)

Medical history
Physical examination
Audiometry
Electrocardiogram
Chest x-ray
Laboratory studies
  Urinalysis
  Blood analysis
  Immunology
Medical summaries
Psychological data
  Intelligence
  Personality
  Continuous performance
  Mental status
Social history and information
  Role and activity
  Socioeconomic status
  Self-concepts
  Health attitudes
  Social attitudes
  Drug proneness
  Retirement
	Performance
	  Financial independence
	  Social independence
	  Reaction time and accuracy
	  Physical function
	Intrapsychic/social psychologic
	  Life satisfaction
	  Happiness
	  Psychosomatic symptoms
	  Self-concepts
	  Mental status

items listed in these tables reflect the multidisciplinary interests of the Duke longitudinal research team in the biomedical, behavioral, and social scientific aspects of aging processes. While each variable or index is related to some theory or hypothesis about aging processes, this brief introduction to the Duke Longitudinal Studies is not the place for a detailed discussion of the theoretical and conceptual origins of each variable or index, its operationalization, or its measurement. The following chapters, three through six, will illustrate the origins and uses of many of the variables and indices in the investigation of particular substantive issues. The references in these chapters will direct those who are interested in details about operationalization and measurement to published material in which such details appear.

109580

These tables are intended to provide an overview of the kinds of evidence that investigators will find in the data tapes of the Duke Longitudinal Studies. For each variable or index, the documentation in the codebooks for both the first and second study provide not only the coding for each item but also the frequency distribution of responses.

As noted, the data sets and their documentation are in the public domain. They are reported in, maintained by, and are available from the Duke Center's Social Survey Laboratory and Data Archive.

DATA ANALYSIS STRATEGIES

In addition to the usual methods of data analysis such as cross tabulation of variables, comparisons of means and variances, correlation and regression analyses, some special procedures that are particularly useful for the analysis of longitudinal data were used on the two longitudinal studies.

Age, Period, and Cohort Analysis

A cross-sequential design is necessary to separate out the effects of age, period, and cohort; i.e., a design with repeated measures for multiple birth cohorts. While the primary method used for this type of analysis, particularly in the second study, has been described in detail previously (Palmore, 1978), the essential steps can be summarized briefly here:

1. Data must be arranged so that the time interval between times of measurement equals the number of years in each birth cohort.
2. Each of the three types of differences must be measured: *longitudinal* (difference between earlier and later measurements on the same cohort), *cross-sectional* (difference between cohorts at the same point in time), and *time-lag* (difference between earlier measurement on an older cohort and later measurement on a younger cohort).
3. Inferences about the effects contained in these differences are

made recognizing that each difference is composed of two effects: e.g., longitudinal effects include age plus period effects; cross-sectional effects include age plus cohort effects; and time-lag effects include period minus cohort effects. If there are no significant differences observed in any of the comparisons, it is usually safe to infer that there are no age, period, or cohort effects. If there are two significant differences, it is usually safe to assume that there is one and only one of the three effects present; that is, the one which is common to the two significant differences. If there are three significant differences, there may be two unequal effects present or three effects present. In this case, outside evidence or theory is necessary to choose one or the other of these two possibilities.

4. The theoretical explanation of any inferred effects needs to be determined. *Age effects* may be due to biological, psychological, and/or social role changes with age. *Period effects* may be due to changes in the environment, measurements, and/or practice effects associated with repeated measures. *Cohort effects* may be due to genetic shifts and/or the interaction of specific historical situations affecting cohorts at specific ages.

There are other methods that can be used to separate age, period, and cohort effects under certain conditions with certain assumptions, such as the multiple regression method of Mason and Mason (1973). This method was used, e.g., to separate age, period, and cohort effects in some analyses of longitudinal personality data (George, Siegler & Okun, 1981). Analysis of variance has also been used to separate period effects from age or cohort effects on personality (Siegler, George & Okun, 1979). Although techniques of statistical analysis of longitudinal data have advanced significantly in the past decade, a number of problems remain (see, e.g., Botwinick & Siegler, 1980; Maddox and Wiley, 1976; Maddox and Campbell, 1985).

Residual Change Analysis

A major problem in longitudinal analysis is determination of the best way to measure individual changes with aging. A number of statisticians have noted that using simple change scores is problematic because interpretation of observed differences between earlier and later scores on variables of interest is difficult. The difficulty has at least two sources:

1. "A regression to the mean" effect illustrated by the fact that persons with higher scores will tend to change in a downward direction and persons with lower scores will tend to change upward; and
2. The potential for errors in measurement is increased when change scores are used because there are two calculations of the measure involved.

One solution to both of these problems is the method of residual change analysis. In this method, a regression analysis is performed in which the score on the second administration of the measure is the dependent variable, and the score on the first administration is the first independent variable. This has the effect of controlling for initial level of the variable of interest, thus eliminating the effects of regression to the mean; this procedure also reduces measurement error caused by the potential doubling of errors in a change score. Second and subsequent variables introduced in the regression equation then are related only to the residual change in the measure, because initial level has been controlled.

Repeated Measures Analysis

An alternative to residual change analysis is a variation of repeated measures analysis of variance (Palmore, Cleveland, Nowlin, Ramm & Siegler, 1979). In this method, the values for dependent variables at each round of observation for which data are available are treated as responses to events and circumstances impinging on individual panelists. An event, such as widowhood or retirement, for example, can then be treated as the independent variable. Since more than one measure of dependent variables might occur before or after an event of interest, a more precise measure of the variable surrounding an event for each subject is required and, in the longitudinal studies, is available. Repeated measures analysis, as used in the Duke studies, differs from traditional repeated measures analysis of variance in that occurrence of an event is represented by a step function occurring in the interval of the event. Adjustment for background characteristics (such as, e.g., resources available to an individual) was accomplished by dividing the population into groups according to high and low scores. Adjustment for the pattern that would have occurred in the absence of an event was made by estimating a time of measurement effect for all subjects. The advantage of this method is that it uses all the available data, including the measures immediately before and after an event. The disadvantage of this method is that it does not control for the regression toward the mean effects.

Special Statistical Problems and Solutions: An Ancillary Study

In an ancillary study, Max Woodbury, a mathematical statistician participating on the longitudinal research team, identified and proposed solutions for three basic problems in data analysis encountered in large longitudinal studies. The first problem, missing data, is a common problem that as recently as a decade ago did not have a commonly accepted solution. The other two problems—the ordering of variables in regression analysis and identification of significant clusters of individuals with similar characteristics—occur when, as in the case of the Duke studies initially, adequate theoretical models of aging processes are not available.

Estimation of Missing Values

The experience of the Duke research indicates that for most panelists, data for most variables over time can be secured. However, even under the best conditions, some protocols lack one or more values for one or more variables at any round of observation. The reasons for this are as varied as unintentional omission in coding or insufficient time to complete a test. For example, in the second study, an estimated 2 percent of the values overall were missing (Palmore, et al., 1979). To illustrate the practical consequences of this, if one omits all cases with missing values on any variable in a multivariate longitudinal analysis, substantial reduction of the number of cases available for analysis results.

In the past, some research investigators have solved this source of potential bias by inserting the group mean score for the missing data. The disadvantage of this method is that it artificially inflates measures of association between variables. A refinement of this method is to insert the mean scores of some subgroup based on such characteristics as age and sex. This increases the accuracy of the estimation but still artificially inflates correlations.

In order to avoid these biases, a missing data estimation program was developed using "the missing information principle." The proposed solution predicts the most likely value for missing scores, based on recursive linear regressions on all the other variables in the data set (Woodbury & Dowdy, 1976; Cleveland, Hamilton, and Ramm, 1978). This procedure provides the most accurate estimation possible on the basis of available data and avoids artificial inflation of correlations when independent and dependent variables are treated as separate data sets.

Markov Network Analysis

In stepwise regression analysis some variables are observed to enter the analysis consistently, other variables not. This fact is frequently ignored or its potential significance is not pursued. Similarly, in path analysis, the ordering of variables in causal sequence is a critical decision for which no formal procedure exists. Markov network analysis provides a possible solution for both problems. Findings from the application of the advantage of this procedure over standard regression analysis in clarifying causal relationships have been illustrated in analyses of data from the Duke Longitudinal Studies (see, e.g., Woodbury, Manton, and Siegler, 1982).

Typology Modelling: Grade of Membership

Grade of membership (GOM) analysis is a statistical model originally developed to deal with problems in assessing medical diagnoses. The logical structure of the GOM, however, has several properties that make it applicable to longitudinal analysis of aging processes where there are multiple categorical variables.

There are two particular features of GOM that distinguish it from most other types of categorical data analysis. The first is that it provides a simultaneous solution to the "taxonomic" and "discriminant" problems. The taxonomic problem involves the identification of clusterings or groups of individual cases. A common approach to this problem is cluster analysis or Q mode factor analysis. Neither approach has proved fully satisfactory because of a lack of a rigorous statistical model to evaluate the outcome of any analysis. The discriminant problem involves the identification of the optimal weighting of a set of variables to discriminate between two or more groups. In discriminant analysis, the groups must be specified a priori and assumed to be "fixed" (i.e., not subject to error).

In the GOM model the taxonomic and discriminant problems are resolved by estimating simultaneously two different types of coefficients using maximum likelihood. The first set of coefficients relates each case to one of a set of K underlying "states." That is, the coefficients describe how distant each case is from each of the K states or pure types. Derived simultaneously is a second set of coefficients which represents the probability of a given type of response for each of the K states. Thus, while the coefficients for individuals describe how the cases are distributed between each of the K states, the coefficients for the responses help to describe what each of the K states signify in terms of the variables employed in the analysis.

The second distinctive feature of the GOM is that coefficients relate each of the cases to each of the pure types. There are K such coefficients for an individual and they are constrained to sum to 1.0 for each person. What makes GOM different from cluster analysis is the possibility that a case may belong to *two or more* pure types—and to differing degrees. In cluster analysis, each case can logically be in only *one* of the groups of clusters. The alternative assumption of GOM is important for several reasons.

First, because a case can fall between two or more groups, it is possible for GOM to represent gradations in the location of a subject on a scale of measurement or partial attainment of a particular state. Second, it offers the possibility of making the GOM model somewhat less sample-dependent than cluster analysis. This occurs because the K pure types represent extreme profiles of characteristics between which cases may be distributed. In terms of clinical diagnosis, for example, pure types might be argued to represent "textbook case" manifestations of a particular disease or condition. Thus, in applying GOM to multiple study populations, one could allow individual cases in each study population to be differently distributed between the pure types yet, by fixing the coefficients relating the variables to the K pure types, maintain identical definitions of the pure types across the study populations. Third, because each case can relate differently to the K pure type, there is no need to assume that the set of cases being analyzed is sampled from a common population.

GOM has been applied to a number of data sets and problems (Woodbury and Manton, 1982). It has been applied to problems in physical diagnosis, comparison of survey sample data on delinquency, and types of patients in nursing homes. Another application of GOM has been to longitudinal psychological data on reaction time from the first Duke Longitudinal Study (Clive, et al., 1983). The analysis was able to identify various patterns of decline in neurological reaction times. Thus in GOM one is able to identify certain stages in the aging process (by identifying the pure types) and to determine how far the individual has progressed between these aging states (by examining the individual level coefficients).

Longevity Measures

One important outcome of aging processes is mortality or, stated positively, longevity. Conventional mortality table analysis is inappropriate for studies which have small study populations (e.g., the Duke studies). For purposes of the Duke studies, three alternative strategies were developed (see e.g., Palmore & Jeffers, 1971):

1. A *Longevity Index* defined as the number of years a deceased participant survived after initial testing, or the number of years a living participant can be expected to survive after initial testing based on standard life expectancy tables specified by age, race, and sex;

2. A *Longevity Quotient* defined as the Longevity Index divided by the expected number of years to be survived at time of initial examination, again based on appropriate life expectancy

tables which permit controls for the actuarial differences in expected longevity based on age, race, and sex; and

3. A *Longevity Difference* defined as the number of years actually survived after initial testing minus the expected number of years to be survived based on age, race, and sex of the participant (Palmore, 1981). This index controls for age, race, and sex differences in expected longevity as does the Longevity Quotient, but it has the advantage of being directly interpretable as the number of years survived in addition to (or less than) the expected number of years.

DATA MANAGEMENT AND COMPUTING PROCEDURES

The Duke Longitudinal Studies span several decades in which remarkable changes have taken place in the way research data are managed and processed using computers. The studies began in days before computers were routinely used in university research. The changes observed in computer technology ensured some complications for Duke investigators and necessitated adaptation to changing capabilities of data management. However, in spite of the demands for continuous adaptation to advances in the art of data processing, the data of the Duke Longitudinal Studies are now publicly available in a form that make them convenient for analysis with modern computing hardware and software.

As is often the case in studies that cover extended periods of time, initial documentation of procedures that, at first, depended partially on oral traditions became more formal and systematic. The following paragraphs outline the data management procedures of the Duke studies and some of the solutions to the problems encountered. While data storage and retrieval lack glamour, in the experience of the Duke research team these tasks are critically important in longitudinal research. For this reason, procedures that worked well at Duke are reported in some detail. Experience in the use of statistical consultation also warrants special attention.

Data Reduction, Cleaning, Storage, and Retrieval

Reduction and Cleaning

A detailed report on *data reduction and cleaning* was published in the appendix of *Normal Aging II* (Palmore, 1974). Some of the issues discussed can be highlighted here. Normally, the data for the Longitudinal Studies were collected on forms completed either by the subject or by technicians working with the subject. Data were entered into the computer system directly from these forms, mostly using a keypunch. Omitting the intermediate step of transcription to special coding forms, which is often used, eliminated a potential source of human errors. The information from these coding forms was keypunched and verified. Verification was accomplished by actually punching the data twice, independently, preferably by two different data entry persons. The two resulting decks were then compared with a Duke Center computer program (VERY) which identified discrepancies for correction by reference to the original data forms. More information on VERY and the two programs described below is available in a technical report on Data Screening Programs (Ramm, 1980).

The verified data then went through several automated cleaning procedures. These useful procedures were designed to detect many of the errors that ordinarily slip by. Details of the programs used in this type of procedure are available in two technical reports "A Model for Error Detection in Medium Sized Data Bases" and "Error Detection in Longitudinal Studies of Aging" (Ramm & Cleveland, 1980 a & b). In brief, the principal points in these reports are:

1. Medium sized but expensive multidisciplinary data bases require almost heroic efforts to avoid loss of data on key variables; automatic editing techniques that can be used on large scale social survey data are not suitable. Specific procedures are required to deal with missing data and data that would be routinely rejected if usual automatic deletion procedures are used.

2. Longitudinal data should be screened in three ways in addition to validity checks: by comparing within variables across

subjects at fixed time (traditional cross-sectional check for outliers); by comparing within subjects at fixed times for feasible relationships among variables; and by comparing changes over time within subjects and within variables.

One automated program (VALID) checked the variables for the obvious error of "being out of range" or for continuous variables dramatically different from the values observed for average of subjects. Additional checks were made with another program (DIFER) which took advantage of the fact that in longitudinal data certain constraints on data over time could be checked. For example, subjects should not be getting younger nor much shorter. Various other forms of continuity in variables could be checked.

Data Storage

The physical storage procedures for large data sets involved the following considerations. Large quantities of data require the use of magnetic tapes. Disk space is usually too expensive for this kind of storage initially and, over time, the size of records becomes too large for disk usage. Codebooks that provide essential documentation must be kept for each wave in the studies (11 for the First Longitudinal, 4 for the Second Longitudinal) and must be carefully related to the original data collection forms. Additional notes and comments by responsible investigators over time must be added to illuminate any problems encountered in data analysis. Security of the data must be insured by having backups of both the tapes and updated codebooks. Backup copies of the codebooks and the tapes were kept at physically different sites to protect against fire loss. Confidentiality of records must be insured by having no obvious identifiers stored on the data files. In the Duke studies, data forms were kept in locked filing cabinets which were in locked offices.

Data Retrieval

In the absence of data analysis computer software appropriate for large scale longitudinal research in 1955, TSAR (Duke Computation Center, 1974) was developed at Duke University in the early 1960s at the request and with the cooperation of the Aging Center.

Even today TSAR is one of the few software packages that conveniently handles the large data records involved for each subject in the Duke Longitudinal Studies. Primary data storage and retrieval, consequently, is still done with TSAR. Files are also created from TSAR which can be accessed by some of the more modern statistical packages such as SPSS (Nie, Hull, Jenkins, Steinbrenner & Bent, 1975) and SAS (SAS Institute, 1979).

For data analysis, an investigator typically selects a subset of all the variables collected for a particular research analysis using SPSS or SAS. This subfile is then stored on disks and used with the SAS or SPSS statistical packages as well as with some of the more specialized packages such as ECTA, MANOVA, and GENCAT. In addition, some forms of analysis are performed with custom-designed programs. An example is the analog-to-digital converter programs to process the Continuous Performance Task (CPT) data (see Chapter Four).

Use of Statistical Consultation

The Duke longitudinal research team did not initially have a full-time statistical consultant. Statistical consultation was typically arranged on an *ad hoc* basis with mathematicians interested in statistics but with little or no experience in longitudinal research. Ensuring continuity of consultation and the interest of the consultants proved to be very difficult. Consequently, in the late 1960s, a full-time statistician specifically for the longitudinal studies was recommended; and, since 1972, a full-time statistician and several part-time consultants with experience in longitudinal data analysis have been available to the Center's Computing and Statistical Laboratory. The investment has been a good one.

The presence of experienced statistical consultants has ensured the availability and accessibility of experts to design data analysis procedures and to help with the potentially complex multivariate analysis of the time-series data. In fact, the general statistical milieu of the Center as a whole was improved by informal as well as formal contacts with competent resident statistical consultants. On recommendation of team statisticians, the SAS package was elected as the most promising and generally most useful for Aging Center use, although SPSS also continued to be popular with investigators. The wisdom of the selection of the SAS package has been confirmed by the fact that the use of SAS in the United States and internationally has increased by five-fold since Duke began using it and it is the fastest growing statistical package in the world.

A USER'S GUIDE TO THE DATA SETS, CODEBOOKS, AND TECHNICAL REPORTS

The data of the Duke Longitudinal Studies are stored and are available for distribution on magnetic tapes through the Center's Data Archive which maintains a number of data sets, many of them documenting longitudinal studies of special relevance for research in aging. Experienced staff of the related Survey Data Laboratory are available for consultation on both technical and substantive issues related to these data sets.

Each data record for each subject in the Duke Longitudinal Studies is stored in an externally readable EBCDIC format so that it can be accessed by any modern statistical package using the appropriate description of the location of variables from the codebooks. The data from each of the two longitudinal studies are stored on separate tapes. Tapes can be prepared which can be used directly with either SAS or SPSS without having to enter the column or position information from the codebooks. This will allow access to the variables by just using the names specified in the codebooks for the SAS or SPSS programs. These derived tapes meet specific requirements of certain statistical analytic packages. This procedure, for example, will simplify use by investigators preferring either SAS or SPSS.

Although various aspects of the longitudinal studies have been published in the various scientific journals familiar to specialists involved in longitudinal studies, many of the detailed procedures for data analysis developed over the years have also been preserved in technical reports maintained in the Duke Center's Survey Data Laboratory and Archive. A Technical Report Series for the longitudinal study has developed and a listing of these technical reports is found in Table 2.7.

The codebooks of the Duke Longitudinal Studies are "living documents" with codes, annotations, and corrections added over time as investigators recorded their experience in data analysis. Cumulatively, this experience has produced current codebooks that document the data sets adequately. Special computer software was created to allow the generation of these codebooks so that future revisions can be made with a minimal amount of tedious and repetitious manual effort.

Codebooks of the Duke studies are organized by study and wave. While many of the variables are repeated from wave to wave, as is appropriate for a longitudinal study, there are some variations. These changes are properly noted. The codebook produced, therefore, should be relatively error free although this conclusion will have

Table 2.7. Technical Reports on the Duke Longitudinal Studies Data Sets

"User's Guide to Missing Data Estimation"
  W. P. Cleveland, R. D. Hamilton, and D. Ramm

"Duke Longitudinal Studies: EEG"
  E. W. Busse and H. S. Wang

"Duke Longitudinal Studies: Psychiatric Data"
  H. S. Wang

"Participation Pattern in Psychological Data for
Longitudinal I"
  I. Siegler and K. Paulig

"Data Screening Programs"
  D. Ramm

"A Model for Error Detection in Medium Sized Data Bases"
  D. Ramm and W. P. Cleveland

"Error Reduction in Longitudinal Studies of Aging"
  D. Ramm and W. P. Cleveland

"Stress and Adaptation in Later Life: Analysis"
  W. P. Cleveland and D. Ramm

to be confirmed by use. As noted previously, a fully documented data set for the Second Longitudinal Study is available. The larger, more complex data set of the First Longitudinal Study may be accessed but at this time access requires special arrangements.

PRESERVATION OF THE ORIGINAL PROTOCOLS

The completed protocols of the longitudinal studies required approximately 20 five-drawer filing cabinets for storage. While preservation of complete protocols is important, this form of storage is costly and inefficient. Consequently, complete protocols have been microfilmed for long term storage. A Kodak process has been used. The procedure involves committing a copy of all protocols and related records to 16 mm microfilm. The microfilm camera used allowed two rolls of film to be exposed simultaneously with identical copies of each image. One copy of the film has been inserted into microfiche jackets for easy access; the other copy is retained in a different location to ensure security. For each wave and for each subject identified only by a subject number a microfiche exists which allows simple access to images of the original documents. These can be stored in considerably less space than the large filing cabinets, with approximately 8,000 microfiche containing all of the information from these studies. The complete protocols of the Duke studies can be conveniently accessed using standard microfiche readers. If necessary, one can obtain reader-printers which can reverse the process and print full-size sheets of paper from microfiche. Duplicate microfiche also can be produced as necessary.

3

The Aging Central Nervous System: Electroencephalographic, Psychiatric, and Medical Findings

The Duke Longitudinal Studies of Aging grew from the initial curiosity of a scientific investigator in changes in the electrical activity of the human brain with age, in the identification of normal in contrast to pathological changes, and in the causes and consequences of these changes. The systematic research which followed spun a large and complex web of connections among the functioning central nervous system, the physical status of the organism, cognitive functioning and ultimately the functioning of individuals in the context of social environment. It is appropriate, therefore, to begin the first chapter highlighting substantive findings with a report of electroencephalographic (EEG) research from which the Duke Longitudinal Studies grew and to present the complementary psychiatric and biomedical research stimulated by the CNS investigations.

Subsequent chapters will illustrate the logical broadening of the research perspective in the longitudinal studies to include behavioral and social factors which contribute to the understanding of norma-

tive aging processes. From the beginning of the Duke Longitudinal
Studies, review of highlights in this chapter indicates, the interconnectedness of aging processes was understood.

ELECTROENCEPHALOGRAPHIC (EEG) FINDINGS

The Problem

In 1948, E. W. Busse's research on epileptic seizures with temporal lobe
localization in adults suggested that many elderly persons referred
for clinical diagnostic EEGs showed focal electrical disturbances aris-
ing from the temporal region of the brain. The focal disturbance
found in elderly subjects was very similar to that encountered in diagnosed epileptics who were part of a research project. The majority of the elderly persons, referred for EEG examinations because
they were believed to have organic brain disease, were free of seizures. Consequently, a number of the EEG interpretations include
the notation: "The focal abnormality present in the record does not
appear to be related to the patient's complaint or to the diagnosis."

  This relatively common focal dysrhythmia in elderly persons had
not been described in the scientific literature and it was evident that
the lack of knowledge regarding EEG changes in late life was seriously limiting the diagnostic value of the EEG interpretation.

  In 1951, a proposal to the National Institutes of Health to study
"the effect of aging upon the central nervous system" was submitted and funded. The research proposed was to be both physiological
and psychological; its major objectives were to standardize the normal electroencephalogram for persons 60 years of age and older and
to establish a basis for distinguishing between normal and pathologic
changes in EEG functioning with age. A preliminary report of findings in 1952 noted "37.3 percent of the old people show focal disturbances in their EEGs (primarily in the left temporal area)" and
"23.3 percent have a combination of diffuse and focal changes with
13.3 percent showing only diffuse dysrhythmias." A detailed report
appeared in the *American Journal of Psychiatry* (Busse, 1954).

  Research on the standardization of the normal EEG for elderly
persons was continued in a new setting when Dr. Busse and several

colleagues moved to Duke University School of Medicine. Again, with NIH support, they continued to chart the EEG changes common to late life and broadened their focus to include social in addition to psychological factors that might be correlated with this physiological change. This preliminary research stimulated the planning that produced, in 1955, the First Longitudinal Study of Aging at Duke.

Methodology

The EEG recording procedure used initially was developed prior to the development of international standards for electrode placement, recording, and classification and, therefore, warrants brief comment. The EEG recording procedure adopted was based on the official procedure used in the armed forces during World War II. Scalp electrodes were placed symmetrically over the major areas of each hemisphere (frontal, precentral, parietal, occipital, anterior temporal, and posterior temporal), with reference leads on the vertex and ears. Particular attention was given to the location of the anterior temporal electrodes, placed 1½ cm. above the zygomatic arch at a point one-third of the distance between the auditory meatus and external canthus of the eye.

EEGs were recorded on an 8-channel Grass instrument by means of both monopolar and bipolar techniques. A sufficient length of tracing was obtained to ensure an adequate evaluation of the waking state. When possible, drowsiness and natural sleep were also recorded. The possible effects of medication taken by a few of the subjects were considered in evaluating the EEGs. Interpretation of the records was based upon adult standards described by Gibbs and Gibbs (1950) and was made independently by at least two investigators. Comparisons of interpretations on the same subjects revealed 88 percent agreement between investigators. Discrepancies were resolved by joint review and consultation.

In the First Longitudinal Study, relatively complete EEG data are available for 267 persons, 127 males and 140 females. The mean age at the beginning of the study was 70.8 years, and the average age of panel survivors 21 years later was 85.2 years (Busse & Wang, 1979).

Results, Associations, and Implications

The following summary of findings from more than two decades of EEG research in the longitudinal studies is derived from a publication by Busse and Wang (1979).

Alpha Activity and Its Correlates

Slowing of the alpha frequency (8 to 13 c/sec) is the most common change in EEGs recorded after the age of 65 years. Cross-sectional and longitudinal studies have demonstrated a decline in mean alpha frequencies in normal control groups. The frequency declines approximately 0.50 to 0.75 c/sec each decade after age 60. Many observed EEG changes with age appear to reflect the health status of the individual. Therefore, it is plausible that alpha slowing found in apparently healthy elderly subjects is influenced by minimal, perhaps subclinical, pathology.

Sex differences in alpha activity among elderly control subjects have been reported by Mundy-Castle (1962), by Obrist and Busse (1965), and by Obrist (1975). Males tend to have a significantly lower mean alpha frequency than females of comparable age.

The alpha slowing within the normal range of 8 to 13 c/sec found in elderly community subjects in the longitudinal studies is not paralleled by changes in intellectual performance. In comparison with the young, healthy adult's average of 10.0 to 10.5 c/sec considered as baseline, the mean alpha frequency of cognitively normal old subjects is significantly lower, reaching 9.0 to 9.5 c/sec about age 70 and 8.5 to 9.0 c/sec after age 80 (Obrist, 1979). In comparison, the observed decline is greater among institutionalized aged patients, particularly those with cerebral vascular disease or neurologic disorders where the frequency is often 8 c/sec or less. Those with obvious dementia usually have frequencies of 7 c/sec or less.

Patients with arteriosclerotic brain disease show not only a slowing of alpha but also a decline in cerebral blood flow and cerebral metabolism. In this type of patient, a number of investigators have reported the degree of slowing correlates with the extent of impaired memory and other impairments of intellectual functioning. This correlation is not consistently found in subjects living in the community. It is possible that some survivors in the community are actually adjusting at a borderline level of brain functioning and may be vulnerable to stress which would precipitate evidence of organic brain disease. There is some clinical evidence that this is true and documenting and measuring the vulnerability of such elderly people deserve attention.

Several studies indicate that there is a relationship between alpha slowing and mortality. This is not surprising when one recognizes the relationship between vascular disease and alpha slowing. Obrist and associates showed that over a span of five to seven years the alpha slowing in those who died was double that found in the survivors. This result has been confirmed by Wang and Busse (1974b) and by Muller et al. (1975).

Theta and Delta (Slow Wave) Activity

In addition to alpha slowing, another common characteristic of EEG changes in late life is the appearance of scattered slow waves. A slight slowing of the alpha index with scattered 6 to 8 c/sec waves is not pathognomonic for any particular disorder. However, a moderate amount of slowing within the theta range (4 to 7 c/sec, delta < 4) and severe slowing (that is, the appearance of delta activity approximately 10 percent of the time) are characteristically found in brain disorders whether they are classified as degenerative or vascular in origin.

Cerebral Metabolism and Brain Function

A correlation has been demonstrated among EEG wave frequency, cerebral oxygen consumption and/or cerebral blood flow (Obrist, Sokoloff, Lassen, Lane, Butler & Feinberg, 1963). The slowing of the dominant EEG frequency in the majority of elderly people appears to be associated with a decline of cerebral metabolism. Diffuse slow activity more than any other EEG indicator is associated with senile intellectual deterioration. Institutionalized elderly subjects manifesting diffuse EEG slowing, for example, exhibit cognitive dysfunction. In contrast, this relationship does not hold for older people living in the community, including those with borderline or mild EEG slowing. It is possible that it is explained by the use of available psychological tests insufficiently sensitive to detect early mental changes (Wang & Busse, 1975).

EEG, blood pressure, and heart disease.   In 1961, a publication appeared linking electroencephalographic changes to blood pressure in a special sample of hospitalized elderly persons (Obrist, Busse & Henry, 1961). When several EEG indicators of brain functioning were plotted separately against mean blood pressure in this group, the incidence of normal EEGs increased markedly as the blood pressure rose, while the number of diffuse slow and mixed normal EEGs were highest when blood pressure readings were lower.

A similar but not identical finding appeared in the First Longitudinal Study. Panelists with a mild elevation of blood pressure tended to present a normal EEG, a finding which suggests that maintaining adequate circulation to the brain may compensate for cerebral arteriosclerotic disease commonly found in older persons.

It was speculated that the diffuse slow activity in many aged psychiatric patients results from the combination of a relatively low blood pressure and cerebral arteriosclerosis (Wang & Busse, 1974a). Wang and Busse explored this speculation in a study that divided subjects from the First Longitudinal Study into four groups: (1) without heart disease, (2) questionable heart disease, (3) definite and compensated heart disease, and (4) definite and decompensated heart disease. This study revealed that the EEG evidence of impaired brain functioning was significantly greater in the subjects with decompensated heart disease when compared to the other three groups. The degree of brain impairment observed, as evidenced by the EEG changes, is probably due to a profound reduction of cerebral blood flow which is shown to be proportional to the reduction in cardiac output. Subjects with compensated heart disease also had a mild hypertension. These findings suggest that mild hypertension in some elderly patients may help to maintain the blood flow to the brain and hence to preserve the status of the brain, perhaps at the expense of the heart. Sustained severe hypertension, however, is often associated with intellectual decline (Wilkie & Eisdorfer, 1961).

Focal EEG abnormalities.   The relatively high percentage of elderly people with focal EEG disturbances predominantly over the temporal areas of the brain was first observed in 1949, reported informally in 1953 and subsequently published in 1954 (Busse, Barnes, Silverman, Shy, Thaler & Frost). In this research, three series of community subjects separated according to socioeconomic criteria were used. A negative correlation was found between the incidence of focal EEG disturbances and lower socioeconomic status, a finding possibly explained by the relatively poorer health status associated with lower socioeconomic status. However, an incidence of focal disturbances of 30 to 40 percent among apparently healthy people has been repeatedly observed, predominately on the left side of the brain. An even higher incidence of abnormal focal slowing (50 percent) was reported by Mundy-Castle (1962) among subjects who were residents of an old age home. The Mundy-Castle report agreed with earlier reports by Busse and colleagues indicating that maximum focal slowing was likely to be found in the anterior temporal area and that 75 percent of these foci were found on the left side. A comparison of Duke longitudinal panelists with aged psychiatric patients indicated that mentally ill older patients have a wider distribution of temporal disturbances with the abnormalities extending into the posterior and mid-temporal areas. Among patients with organic brain syndrome, the abnormal focal changes often took the form of localized accentuated diffuse slow activity (Barnes, Busse & Friedman, 1956). These initial observations and conclusions have not been altered over the years. Focal slow activity in the anterior temporal area is compatible with a good social adjustment and cognitive functioning in old age. However, when slowing involves adjacent areas or is associated with a more diffuse disturbance, organic brain syndrome is probable.

Temporal abnormalities and age of onset.   Kooi and associates (1964) reported increased incidence of temporal lobe disturbances with advancing age. Shortly thereafter, Busse and Obrist (1965) made a similar report using a special sample of volunteer subjects, including some from the longitudinal studies. The age of subjects ranged from 20 to 80 years. Foci were found in the EEG recordings of 3.4 percent of subjects 20 to 29 years of age, 8 percent between 30 and 39, 20 percent between 40 and 49, 22 percent between 50 and 59, and 36 percent between 60 and 69 years of age with a very gradual increase thereafter (Busse, 1973).

Dominant Background Activity and the Presence of Foci

From a cross-sectional analysis early in the First Duke Longitudinal Study, EEGs with a dominant alpha rhythm were found in 61 percent of the subjects. Sixteen percent exhibited low voltage fast activity. Fifteen percent were *diffuse fast* and 7 percent *diffuse slow* activity.

The age distribution in relation to dominant activity among these subjects (average age about 70 years) indicated that younger subjects accounted for 75 percent of the *diffuse fast* activity but were under-represented in the *diffuse slow* category. The mean age of subjects in the *diffuse fast* category was 66.7 years, in the *diffuse slow* category 77.7 years. Subjects with *dominant alpha* and *low voltage fast* frequencies were found throughout the age range and were equally divided between those over and under 70 years of age.

Among those with foci, 75 percent of subjects with *diffuse slow* EEGs had foci, 38 percent of those with *dominant alpha*, and 25 percent of those exhibiting *diffuse fast* activity. None of the *low voltage fast* EEGs contained focal disturbances (Wang & Busse, 1969).

Activation of Temporal Foci

Hyperventilation tends to exacerbate temporal slowing in subjects who exhibit it but does not elicit new focal activity. Tilting of a subject starting from a prone position does not exacerbate foci or elicit new ones. Five percent inhalation of CO_2 does not eliminate or reduce the severity of observed temporal foci. Temporal foci are not reduced or eliminated while the subject is exposed to hyperbaric conditions, and there is no evidence of a change following hyperbaric exposure (Obrist & Busse, 1972). Drowsiness does increase the appearance of foci (Obrist, 1976).

Psychological Implications of Age-related EEG Changes

Psychological deficiencies have been suspected as concomitants of age-related changes in EEG but have not been unequivocally confirmed. In one investigation involving panelists in the First Duke Longitudinal Study, an EEG focus predominantly in the left temporal region was significantly associated with a decline in verbal but not performance ability as measured by WAIS. This decline in verbal ability over a span of approximately two and a half years was greater in the focal group than in the nonfocal group (Wang, Obrist & Busse, 1970). In another special study, however, again involving 20 subjects from the same panel selected because they displayed severe temporal foci and 20 aged-matched cases having normal EEGs, no differences could be found in learning or memory. Survival 12 years later was approximately equal in the two groups (Obrist, 1975).

Fast Activity

In the analysis of EEG data in the Duke Longitudinal Studies, fast waves above the alpha range are distinguished from low voltage fast activity on the basis of amplitude and, to some degree, by regularity of pattern. The frequency of fast activity is confined to a relatively narrow spectrum, and its amplitude usually exceeds 25 microvolts. The original Gibbs classification was the initial basis for all interpretations. Fast activity is differentiated as *F1* and *F2*. Evaluation of F1 includes determination of amplitude and frequency of *fast activity*, the percent of time it is present, and the number of leads in which it appears. F2 identifies an excessive amount of *diffuse fast activity*.

In the First Longitudinal Study as well as in other investigations, the amount of fast activity present in normal females increases in young adulthood, reaches a peak at late middle life, and then gradually declines. Fast activity appears predominantly over the precentral areas of both hemispheres and is rarely associated with "Mu" rhythms. In special studies, Busse and Obrist (1965) have noted that women between the ages of 20 and 39 years have a prevalence of 8 percent fast activity. Between the ages of 40 and 59 the prevalence of such activity increases to 26 percent, but thereafter does not increase. After age 60 and until age 79, the prevalence is 23 percent. After the age of 80, the amount of fast activity observed in the EEG recordings of females appears to begin a gradual decline. The possible role of hormonal changes in the development of fast rhythms in middle-aged women has been suggested by McAdam, Tait, and Orme (1957), who observed a significantly greater amount of fast activity in post- as opposed to pre-menstrual women. The relationship between menopause and EEG activity warrants further study.

Thompson and Wilson (1966) conclude that fast activity is associated with superior learning. Obrist (1976) adds that the presence of fast activity in the EEGs of the elderly persons "can probably be regarded as a favorable sign,'' affecting both longevity and mental capacity. In contrast, fast activity is rarely found in deteriorated senile patients.

Summary: Aging and EEG Findings

Three principal objectives were fulfilled in longitudinal study of EEG patterns and EEG changes in later life. First, normative patterns of EEG activity and changes in this activity with age in later life, previously unavailable, were characterized systematically, with particular attention given to characterizing alpha, theta and delta activity and to focal disturbances. Second, the importance of distinguishing age-related changes in EEG activity (which for the most part was found to be benign) and pathological change was confirmed. Third, the identified pathological changes in EEG patterns are associated with, and possibly explained in part, by changes in cardiovascular function and, more generally, by evidence of declining health status. Pathological changes are also associated with consequential changes in cognitive functioning generally, although age-related changes in EEG activity generally are not associated with decline in cognitive functioning.

THE AGING CENTRAL NERVOUS SYSTEM: PSYCHIATRY

The Problem

The psychiatric observations included in the First Longitudinal Study were influenced by the clinical experiences and responsibilities of the psychiatrists involved in the study and by their major interest in psychosomatic medicine. Three common categories of mental disorders are particularly significant for clinicians serving older adults: depression, hypochondriasis, and organic brain disease. Of secondary importance are anxiety reactions, paranoid conditions, and sleep disorders.

Psychiatric observations frequently provide insights that are useful in developing meaningful clinical approaches, and, such observations become particularly valuable when correlated with other information such as the physical status of individuals and their psychosocial situation (Busse, Dovenmuehle & Brown, 1960). The findings from the Duke Longitudinal Studies illustrate the relevance of research for therapeutic approaches to problems in later life as evidenced in a number of publications (e.g., Busse, 1956). Note also the following examples:

> Guilt is not an important psychic determinant of depression in elderly persons and is not the major cause of feelings of depression. Depression is more often related to the loss of self-esteem because of feelings of inferiority (Busse, Barnes, Silverman, Thaler & Frost, 1954).

> Social stress is particularly relevant to the appearance of hypochondriasis in late life. Unless the social stress is alleviated, improvement is unlikely (Busse, 1976).

> Clinicians report that depressive symptoms are common in patients with organic brain disease and complicate diagnostic procedures. The majority of clinical studies indicate that depressive symptoms are more common in cerebral arteriosclerosis and cerebral vascular brain disease disturbances than in senile dementia. One explanation is that personal insight is less frequently observed in senile dementia (Busse, 1978).

Depression: Measurement and Findings

Some years ago, depression in the elderly was often considered "prodromal depression" or the "neuroasthenic stage" of cerebral arteriosclerosis or senile dementia. Post (1962) and other investigators demonstrated that elderly diagnosed as depressed do not subsequently develop cerebral degeneration more often than do elderly people in general. The prevalence of depression in later life was investigated in great detail in the First Longitudinal Study which included a clinical psychiatric evaluation (see, e.g., Gianturco & Busse, 1978). The panelists in this study, it is important to note, were selected because they were functioning in the community, not because of suspected psychiatric problems. At the first observation 21% of the panelists were clinically diagnosed to be depressed. In the final round of observations almost two decades later, 25% of the surviving panelists were so diagnosed. In the intervening eight observations the estimated prevalence ranged between 15% and 29% with the average being 21%. For panelists seen as many as 7 or 8 times by psychiatric clinicians over the course of the study only 30% were never diagnosed as depressed, 40% had only one depressive episode and the remaining 30% had two or more episodes. Panelists between the ages of 60 and 70 were slightly less likely to experience depressive episodes, but after age 70 the prevalence of depressive episodes (about 21%) was relatively constant for 70, 80, and 90 year olds. Given the sampling procedure for assembling the panel, one should generalize observed prevalence rates with caution. However, the more one emphasizes the elite characteristics of the panel and acknowledges that survival over time in such a longitudinal panel accentuates eliteness, the more impressively high the observed rates of diagnosed depression in later life appear to be.

Depressed elderly patients occasionally present a clinical picture of pseudodementia. Obviously the proper recognition of a depressive disorder is essential for clinical purposes because a depressed older person might appear to be demented. Depression, however, has relatively little importance as a causal factor in organic brain disease when evidence from the first Duke study is considered.

Wang and Busse (1971) have reported in some detail observations regarding dementia in old age. In this study, the term *brain impairment* was utilized to designate measures of loss of brain function based on a number of laboratory procedures including EEG, measures of cerebral blood flow, and cerebral metabolism. The manifestations of possible brain impairment were also determined by psychological tests, clinical measures of intellectual performance, and observed emotional variations. A poor correlation between these two types of evaluation (laboratory procedures and clinical observations) was found. Of particular interest is the discrepancy, as great as 25 percent (Busse & Wang, 1974a), found in the classification of patients and subjects exhibiting a precipitous decline in clinically observable mental signs and symptoms without evidence of physiological brain changes. Careful consideration of factors such as general physical health, economic status, social environment, and previous living habits led to the conclusion that dementia during late life is a socio-psycho-somatic disorder.

Organic Brain Syndrome:
Measurement and Findings

The technique of assessment for organic brain syndrome (OBS) in the First Longitudinal Study was a systematic mental status examination using two protocols to rate the presence or absence and the degree of organic signs and symptoms. The evaluator completed a six-point OBS rating scale utilizing all observations made during the mental examination. A discrepancy between the elderly person's subjective self-assessment of abilities and the more objective clinical evaluations of impairment appeared frequently. Gianturco and Busse (1978) have reported, for example, that many elderly subjects complain of memory decline or intellectual impairment yet perform adequately on tests of these mental functions.

During the first series of observations 20 percent of the panel reported poor memory for recent events. In addition, 6 percent said they had a poor memory for remote events, and 10 percent considered themselves to have had a decline in intellectual function, particularly in such areas as problem-solving. However, in contrast to this, of the 36 percent of the panelists who had subjective misgivings about cognitive functioning, only 14 percent of the panelists were classified in clinical evaluations as having problems of orientation, particularly with time and date, and just 3 percent demonstrated some confusion. Further, evaluations for organic disability as summarized in Table 3.1 indicate that at the initial observation in the first study 26 percent were considered to show evidence of possible to mild organic signs and symptoms, whereas 3 percent were rated as having moderate to serious disability.

The discrepancy between subjective reports and clinical assessments, which has become more apparent over the course of the longitudinal studies, indicates that panelists complain about more extensive decline in cognitive abilities than the structured clinical evaluations demonstrate. It is of interest that panelists classified as moderately to severely disabled by OBS represented 3 percent of the sample initially. This percentage is not remarkably different from the prevalence of organic brain syndrome reported in the epidemiological literature.

Table 3.1. Prevalence of Organic Brain Syndrome

Round	No Disability	Mild Disability	Moderate to Severe Disability
I	71%	26%	3%
II	78%	17%	4%
III	79%	18%	4%
IV	62%	33%	8%
V	63%	29%	8%
VI	60%	31%	9%
VII	48%	46%	3%
VIII	62%	30%	8%
IX	77%	23%	0%
X	50%	38%	12%

Observed prevalence of mild cognitive disability (less than 20 percent disability) varies by round of observation from a low of 17 percent at the second observation to a high of 46 percent at the seventh observation. There is a tendency for the percentage in the moderate to severe category of disability (greater than 20 percent cognitive disability) to increase from 3 percent at first observation to 12 percent in the tenth observation. These observations cover a period of twenty years. The average age of the sample over this period increased from 70.8 to 85.2 years. Again, this four-fold increase in significant OBS is consistent with other epidemiological findings.

There were 76 subjects who were rated mildly impaired at the initial observation. By the next observation, 32 of these 76 were still rated impaired, 16 were rated unimpaired, 18 were dead, and 10 did not return. During the course of the First Longitudinal Study an additional 39 subjects were rated *impaired* but in a subsequent year were rated *unimpaired*. These findings suggest variability in the course of organic brain syndrome that is unlikely to be explained by measurement error alone. These observations suggest that the signs and symptoms of organic brain disease are not inevitably persistent but rather are characterized by varying degrees of remission and exacerbations.

Longitudinal analysis of all subjects over the course of two decades revealed that 154 (59 percent of the panelists) eventually receive an evaluation indicating the presence of organic brain syndrome with some degree of disability before death or dropout from the panel. This life course prevalence rate is much higher than would be indicated by any cross-sectional analysis of the presence or absence of dementia. To state it another way, from our longitudinal data an episode involving at least some brain impairment occurred for roughly half the elderly in the study who had survived to their 60th birthday and beyond. Again, while generalizing this rate from panel evidence is not indicated, such a lifetime prevalence rate in a sample drawn from community rates is very high.

The factors contributing to the appearance of organic brain signs and symptoms in the first longitudinal panel studied by Busse and Wang (1974a) identified the major risk factors to be decompensated heart disease, low socioeconomic status, and decreased physical and mental activity. Social isolation was not, as Lowenthal (1965) reported earlier, a significant risk factor. The findings from Lowenthal's San Francisco project concluded that isolation may well be a consequence rather than a causal factor in the development of organic mental illnesses in old age.

The relationship of OBS to cardiovascular pulmonary disease was examined very carefully in the first study. Mild elevation of blood pressure was found to be positively correlated with preservation of adequate brain function. One may speculate that the relatively high blood pressure may be necessary to maintain sufficient blood supply to the brain for adequate cerebral function (Busse & Wang, 1974b). A similar observation was made in the previous section of this chapter to the relationship between blood pressure and brain functioning as measured by EEG procedures.

THE BIOLOGICAL CONTEXT OF CNS AGING

The Problem

Biomedical data collected in the two Duke Longitudinal Studies suggest some general conclusions about the health-illness continuum among middle aged and older individuals. Interactions between health status and both socioeconomic and behavioral factors can be studied in the two panels to interpret a number of observations about health and illness in the late middle and later years. Moreover, the two biomedical data sets are sufficiently rich that a great deal of "un-mined data" are available for future researchers interested in health and health-related issues posed by individuals as they age.

Methods

The biomedical data are derived from three information sources:

1. Medical history information available for each individual at each visit (by face-to-face interview with a medical internist in the first study, by pencil-and-paper questionnaire in the second study);
2. Physical examination of each panelist at each visit performed by an internist during both studies; and
3. Laboratory and supplemental clinical studies for both studies (the laboratory protocol included routine hemogram, clinical chemistry, electrocardiogram, chest x-ray).

Evaluation of the biomedical data set has focused upon four areas of primary interest:

1. Consideration of atherosclerotic cardiovascular disease (ASCVD) in terms of "risk factors" influential in the advent of myocardial infarction ("heart attack");
2. The role of ASCVD in age-related changes found in cognitive function;
3. Physical health issues unrelated to the cardiovascular system, including studies of the immune system; and
4. Health-related behavior.

Findings from each of these areas of research interest are highlighted below.

Findings

Cardiovascular Functioning

Among middle aged and younger populations, a number of factors have been related to the occurrence of myocardial infarction, a major clinical manifestation of heart disease (ASCVD). Four reports based upon data collected in the two Duke Longitudinal Studies have examined these factors as they relate to occurrence of this illness among older individuals.

Serum cholesterol levels, long recognized to have a potent association with advent of heart attack in younger individuals, appear less associated with this clinical event among individuals over 60 years of age than among adults generally. Older male panelists with clinical and self-reported evidence of atherosclerotic heart disease did not differ in serum cholesterol level when compared with their counterparts free of manifestation of this disease (Nowlin, Eisdorfer & Bates, 1969).

The habit of *cigarette smoking*, another health factor long demonstrated to be keyed to advent of myocardial infarction, was appraised in prospective fashion among older men. A population of older male cigarette smokers was compared to non-smokers (with exclusion of individuals who had terminated the habit). Incidence of myocardial infarction did not differ between those two groups over a six-year interval in the second study (Nowlin, 1978). Cigarette smoking as a risk factor in heart disease appears to be more important in the middle than in the later years.

Obesity, another factor which often is considered a cardiovascular risk factor in adult populations, was evaluated among male panelists in the first study (Nowlin, 1974). Use of the Quetelet scale (weight divided by square of height) served to denote degree of obesity. The male panelists were divided into two groups based upon high (more obese) or low (less obese) scores. Incidence of acute myocardial infarction (as indicated by history and electrocardiographic evidence) was the same in both groups. Age groupings, considered in 10-year cohorts, did not influence this relationship.

Systolic blood pressure level, which has a proven positive association with subsequent occurrence of heart attack, was found to be a risk factor among older male panelists. Perhaps more importantly, personality factors appeared to have a greater effect than blood pressure on the incidence of myocardial infarction as indicated by evidence from the Second Longitudinal Study (Williams, Nowlin & Wilkie, 1973). Again, in a prospective analysis, an association between "anxiety" among older men and the occurrence of myocardial infarction was demonstrated. Older men who experienced the myocardial infarction event scored higher on the Cattell 16-PF ''O-Scale'' (a Cattell personality inventory factor indicative of ''anxiety'') than did older men who did not have this characteristic.

In summary, upon consideration of ''risk factor'' related to acute myocardial infarction among two panels of older subjects, serum cholesterol, cigarette smoking, and obesity seem less influential in their association with this illness than personality factors and systolic blood pressure. Personality factors and systolic blood pressure appear to have and retain a prominent role as ''risk factors'' in the later years as they do in adulthood generally.

Cardiovascular Disease and Cognitive Functioning

The potential role of cardiovascular disease as a prime factor explaining the documented age-related decline in measures of cognitive function has been evaluated among subjects in the second longitudinal panel (Siegler & Nowlin, 1979a). Based upon presence or absence of electrocardiographic evidence of coronary heart disease and/or hypertension as determined by blood pressure recordings, four groupings of cardiovascular disease were defined: (1) a group free of cardiovascular disease; (2) a hypertensive group with no electrocardiographic evidence of atherosclerotic heart disease; (3) a nonhypertensive group with electrocardiographic evidence of atherosclerotic heart disease; and (4) a group with both hypertension and electrocardiographic evidence of atherosclerotic heart disease.

Level of intellectual function among each of these groups was determined by use of the Wechsler Adult Intelligence Scale (WAIS). WAIS scores, averaged over the four observations in the second study, were highest among the second group (hypertension but free of atherosclerotic heart disease). The next highest WAIS score was found among individuals with atherosclerotic heart disease but free of hypertension. The third highest score was noted among the group with no evidence of hypertension or atherosclerotic heart disease. The lowest WAIS score was found among the group with both indicators of cardiovascular disease. However, among the four cardiovascular disease groups, there was no difference in pattern of change in WAIS scores over the six years of study.

These findings imply that cardiovascular disease might well have a role in determining intellectual function in an older population; but the effects of the disease appears to be earlier than the entry age for this particular longitudinal study panel.

Physical Health Indicators and Other Systems

Aortic findings.   Several specialized issues related to clinical manifestation of atherosclerosis were examined from biomedical data collected from the two studies. Two chest x-ray findings suggestive of atherosclerosis in the thoracic aorta—calcification and tortuosity—were considered in terms of coincident clinical atherosclerotic manifestation. Individuals in the second study with both aortic conditions present were more likely to develop myocardial infarction subsequently than individuals free of these conditions.

Arcus senilis.   Further, arcus senilis (a pigment deposition at the limbus of the eye and, at one time, considered to be indicative of coincident atherosclerosis) was evaluated. Individuals in the second study with and without the arcus changes at the first observation were prospectively studied over the three succeeding visits for serum cholesterol level and occurrence of myocardial infarction. Initial cholesterol levels did not differ between the two groups and there was no difference in pattern of change in this blood lipid over the six years of study. Frequency of heart attack did not differ between the group with and without arcus senilis.

Skin changes.   While age-related changes in the cardiovascular system attract a great deal of attention among both health professionals and laity, other health-related issues have considerable importance. Specific changes in skin related to aging have been described (Tindall & Palmore, 1974). Certain skin lesions, when frequent in number, are associated with decreased longevity (e.g., asteatosis, scrotal angiomata, nevi). Various other skin lesions whose functioning has been correlated with increasing age, most notably so-called cherry angiomata and actinic keratoses, appear to be relatively benign (Tindall & Smith, 1970).

Visual acuity.   The well-known age-associated decrement in visual functioning with age has been confirmed in the first Duke study (Anderson & Palmore, 1973). Despite increasing vision problems with age, however, most of the older individuals in the longitudinal panels managed a successful life-style with the assistance of available prosthetics.

Vitamin B-12.   Whanger and Wang (1970) assessed Vitamin B-12 serum levels among participants in the first study. Two issues were examined. First, B-12 was explored as an indicator of nutritional status; second, lower levels of this vitamin were explored, in part, because of a possible association with the occurrence of dementia and psychiatric illness among older individuals. When panelists over 75 years of age were compared to individuals 60–74 years of age, no difference was noted in serum B-12 levels. Also no difference in B-12 level was noted between older individuals with mental illness and those not falling into that diagnostic category.

Immune System Function

As a beginning assessment of the immune system and the aging process, serum immunoglobulin levels were appraised among individuals from both Duke Longitudinal Studies (Buckley & Dorsey, 1970; Buckley, 1980). Cross-sectional studies indicated increasing serum levels of Immunoglobulin IgA and IgG across successive 10-year age cohorts (less than 55 years of age, 55–64, 65–74, and greater than 75 years of age) with decrease in levels of IgM. Longitudinal evaluation of these three immunoglobulins revealed no consistent patterns of change over periods of study as long as ten years. When specific age groups were evaluated for patterns of time-related change, no age-cohort differences were apparent.

Vibratory Sense

As an indicator of integrity of the peripheral sensory nervous system, quantitative measurements of vibratory sense at upper and lower extremities were taken among panelists in the second study (Nowlin, 1980). An instrument delivering a standard vibratory frequency with rheostatvariable intensity was placed at the ankles and wrists to obtain these measurements. As expected and previously demonstrated, an age-difference was evident. Older individuals present less vibratory sensitivity. Likewise, women at all ages demonstrated a lower vibratory threshold than did men. Vibratory threshold measurements were available for a two-year followup; there was a significant decrement in vibratory threshold over this comparatively short time interval.

Health-related Behavior

Anxiety. Interest in the interplay between health and behavioral measures has characterized much of the research strategy underlying both Duke Longitudinal Studies. For example, scientific interest in the interrelationship of the cardiovascular status and intellectual function has been noted earlier. Another interest in age-related health behavior has focused on *anxiety* induced by the physical examination setting (Nowlin, 1974b). This feeling-state was assessed in a subgroup of panelists in the second study at the time of their initial visit. The Nowlis Mood Adjective Checklist (Nowlis, 1956) self-report of mood was administered at three points during the course of the study.

Women reported more anxiety initially than did males; at the third and final assessment women and men were equivalent in anxiety reported. Age did not influence either the absolute level of anxiety reported (as averaged over the three report periods) nor did age affect change in this feeling-state over the course of the study.

Degree of spontaneity with which symptoms were presented was also appraised in semi-quantitative analysis (Nowlin, 1978). Responses to a standardized set of questions about symptoms in each of several organ systems (e.g., cardiovascular, respiratory, musculo-skeletal, gastro-intestinal) were scored in such a way to indicate extent of willingness to provide symptoms spontaneously. Through use of this technique, women were found more spontaneous than men; older panelists were more spontaneous than younger ones. These findings hold even when simultaneously controlling for health status.

Sexuality

Sexuality represents an intersection between health and behavior which has been explored extensively in both longitudinal studies. Reports from the first study (Pfeiffer, Verwoerdt & Wang, 1968; Verwoerdt, Pfeiffer & Wang, 1969; Pfeiffer, 1969) were based upon interview information obtained at each visit. Men, in general, reported higher levels of sexual activity and interest than did women. Both decline and increase in sexuality were reported among panelists with decline, on average, being the rule.

Panelists in the second study were queried in a written health questionnaire about sexual interest and activity. Initial cross-sectional evaluation of responses at the first observation (Pfeiffer, Verwoerdt & Davis, 1972) confirmed earlier findings. Decline in sexual interest and activity was reported as early as the fifth decade, although marked individual variability still typified these self-reports. Evaluation of factors influencing sexuality revealed age and gender to be the most potent. Self-perception of health and global physician rating of health indicated only minimal influences. Longitudinal evaluation of data (George & Weiler, 1980) indicated a remarkable stability of sexual interest and activity over a six-year interval among panelists in the second study.

CEREBRAL BLOOD FLOW (CBF) AND VASCULAR REACTIVITY IN SENESCENCE: AN ANCILLARY STUDY

The Problem

A special supplemental study of central nervous system functioning examined experimentally the blood flow to the brain and the reactivity of those blood vessels to inhalation of CO_2 in several groups of older persons. The specific aims of the experiment involving a special study population which did not include subjects from the longitudinal studies were:

1. To test comparatively the responsiveness of the cerebral vasculature to CO_2 inhalation in well-defined younger and elderly groups, preselected on the basis of physical and mental examinations, and matched for age and sex; and
2. To provide age-specific control data for interpretation of clinical CBF findings, both with respect to regional blood flow pat-

terns under normocapnic conditions (normal tension of CO_2 in blood) and with respect to CO_2 reactivity.

The results of this experiment were expected to clarify whether cerebral vascular response to CO_2 could be used to estimate presence and severity of cerebrovascular disease in elderly persons. Additionally, the data would provide evidence of how feasible it would be to set up a simple model of cerebrovascular disease severity based on CO_2 reactivity. The data would also provide a normative model against which blood flow in older stroke victims could be assessed.

Research Method

The research strategy was to obtain cerebral blood flow (CBF) measurements in six groups of subjects: (1) normal adults (age 21–30); (2) normal elderly (age 55 and older); (3) elderly with dementia but no clinically detectable vascular disease; (4) elderly with uncomplicated hypertension; (5) elderly with peripheral vascular disease (primarily coronary); and (6) elderly with clinically detectable cerebral ischemia. It was hypothesized that groups 1, 2, and 3 would have essentially normal blood flow and reactivity. Group 4 was expected to have lowered CBF and reactivity was not predicted. Group 5 was expected to have reduced CBF and reactivity. Group 6 was expected to show reduced CBF but to have normal reactivity.

The method used has been detailed extensively in several publications (Obrist, Thompson, King & Wang, 1967; Obrist, Thompson, Wang & Cronquist, 1971; Obrist, Silver, Wilkinson, Harel, Heyman & Wang, 1973; Corbett & Eidelman, 1973; Rao, Ali, Omar & Halsey, 1973). In brief, the subject breathed normal air with tracer amounts of Xenon-133 gas for one minute through an anesthesia mask. Blood flow to the brain was then recorded from 8 detectors placed bilaterally over the frontal, central, parietal and temporal regions of the head. Expired isotope and end-tidal CO_2 values along with data from the head detectors were followed for 15 minutes. Arterial blood pressure (BP) was obtained from the brachial artery and four samples of blood gases were also taken over the 15-minute period from the same site. EKG measurements were also included throughout the test period. The CO_2 reactivity test was given after a one-hour delay. This test was identical with the above except for the addition of 5% CO_2 to the inspired gas mixture beginning 5 minutes before CBF measurements were initiated. From the above data, blood flow to grey matter and white matter in the various brain areas can be obtained by computation from a model of known parameters governing brain blood flow.

A total of 106 subjects were studied, using the research protocol initially outlined. Of these, 93 provided usable data (Table 3.2).

Findings

Preliminary analysis of these 93 subjects focused on 8 cerebral blood flow variables: (1) F_1—regional flow of fast compartment (gray matter); (2) F_2—regional flow of slow compartment (white matter, slightly distorted by the contamination of extra cerebral tissues); (3) FF_1—fraction of fast compartment; (4) W_1—relative weight of slow compartment as indicated by the detector; (5) W_2—relative weight of slow compartment equal to $1-W_1$; (6) MF—mean flow, mathematically extrapolated and calculated using the height over area method; (7) f—weighted average flow, calculated from F_1, F_2, W_1, and W_2;

Table 3.2. Number of Experimental Subjects, by Group

	Tested	Reliable Data
	(Number)	
Healthy adults (age 21-30)	22	20
Healthy elderly (55 years or older)	21	20
Elderly with dementia	20	18
Elderly with hypertension	15	13
Elderly with peripheral vascular disease (primarily coronary disease)	13	10
Elderly with cerebrovascular disease	15	12
TOTAL	106	93

and (8) Initial Slope (IS)—mathematically extrapolated and calculated using the first two minutes of the slope of flow indicators.

Three summary variables of vascular reactivity were employed: (1) absolute reactivity (AR); (2) relative reactivity (RR) with respect to the initial flow value; and (3) corrected RR adjusted to pCO_2 values of 40 mmHg. The equations used appear in Table 3.3.

Table 3.4 summarizes the mean end-tidal pCO_2, mean F_1 values of the 8 regions under room air (control) and hypercapnic condition (4–5% CO_2), and the mean absolute reactivity and the mean relative reactivity for the six groups of subjects. The findings clearly support a relationship between cerebrovascular disease and a reduction or impairment of vascular reactivity. The impairment of reactivity to CO_2 is even more apparent when each region is evaluated separately.

Table 3.5 shows the percent of subjects in each experimental group who demonstrated a subnormal vascular reactivity in different regions of the brain. Subjects with cerebrovascular disease (by history or angiographic confirmation) clearly have more impairment of vascular reactivity in several but not all regions of the brain.

Table 3.3. Equations for Calculating Vascular Reactivity

$$\text{Absolute Cerebral Vascular Reactivity (AR)} = \frac{rCBF_H - rCBF_C}{pCO_{2H} - pCO_{2C}} \text{ ml/mmHg}$$

$$\text{Relative Cerebral Vascular Reactivity (RR)} = \frac{AR}{rCBF_C} \times 100 \text{ \%/mmHg}$$

$$\text{Corrected Relative Reactivity (RR}_{40}) = \frac{RR}{1.0 + RR\,(40 - pCO_{2(I)})}$$

rCBF = regional cerebral blood flow (F_1 – flow of fast compartment or gray matter; MF – non-compartmental mean flow; f – weighed mean flow)

C = control of normocapnia

H = hypercapnia

pCO_2 = end-tidal CO_2 saturation determined by a capnograph

I = initial (under room air)

Table 3.4. Summary of Experimental Results

Group	Healthy Adults		Elderly Persons (55 years old or over)			
	1 Normal Aging	2 Normal Old	3 Demented	4 Hypertensive	5 Cardio-vascular	6 Cerebro-vascular
Number of Subjects	20	20	18	13	10	12
Mean End-Tidal pCO_2 (mmHg)						
control	36.9 ± 4.8	30.9 ± 5.2	30.3 ± 3.8	31.4 ± 5.3	31.1 ± 6.8	31.1 ± 4.9
hypercapnia	43.6 ± 4.2	39.3 ± 5.1	37.3 ± 4.3	39.4 ± 3.8	36.7 ± 6.0	36.9 ± 5.7
difference	6.7 ± 2.0	8.5 ± 4.0	7.0 ± 2.5	8.0 ± 4.7	5.6 ± 2.6	5.8 ± 2.2
Mean Arterial Blood Pressure (mmHg)						
control	86.3 ± 3.9	100.8 ± 10.7	100.3 ± 10.4	104.9 ± 15.9	108.7 ± 8.3	104.1 ± 8.1
hypercapnia	86.8 ± 5.0	102.1 ± 10.9	104.3 ± 9.3	111.1 ± 13.2	113.6 ± 17.2	106.3 ± 11.4
Mean rCBF (F_1) of 8 Regions (ml/100gm/min)						
control	73.3	51.3	43.7	49.3	48.2	46.5
hypercapnia	98.9	70.1	60.1	60.7	59.6	54.4
% change	34.9	36.6	39.5	23.0	23.6	16.8
Mean Vascular Reactivity (8 regions)						
absolute (ml/mmHg)	3.92	2.83	2.51	1.35	1.09	1.26
relative	5.46	5.91	5.91	3.67	3.01	3.24

Table 3.5. Percent of Subjects in Different Groups with Subnormal Vascular Reactivity

Cerebral Regions	Right Hemisphere				Left Hemisphere			
	pre-central	post-central	parietal	inf. frontal	pre-central	post-central	parietal	inf. frontal
Absolute Reactivity								
normal limits*	1.76	0.72	1.16	0.72	1.21	0.73	1.30	0.95
elderly subjects								
healthy	40%	5%	20%	10%	25%	10%	26%	5%
demented	28%	0%	19%	11%	22%	6%	19%	22%
hypertensive	69%	23%	39%	15%	39%	23%	46%	46%
cardiovascular	55%	22%	22%	44%	44%	56%	44%	29%
cerebrovascular	60%	30%	50%	80%	50%	50%	70%	56%
Relative Reactivity								
normal limits*	2.00	0.75	1.24	0.61	1.10	0.47	1.42	0.87
elderly subjects								
healthy	20%	0%	10%	5%	5%	0%	5%	0%
demented	6%	0%	6%	0%	17%	0%	6%	6%
hypertensive	46%	31%	15%	15%	15%	15%	31%	27%
cardiovascular	33%	22%	22%	33%	44%	33%	56%	14%
cerebrovascular	60%	20%	30%	40%	30%	40%	30%	56%

* Normal limits are defined as two standard deviations below the mean values obtained from a group of healthy adults aged between 21 and 30 years old.

THE USE OF AUTOPSY IN LONGITUDINAL RESEARCH: AN ANCILLARY STUDY

The Problem

This special ancillary study had two objectives, one practical and one theoretical. Practically, the study was intended to explore the feasibility of bringing to autopsy at the end of the first study the surviving panelists who, with the consent of next-of-kin, agreed to participate; theoretically, assessing the scientific utility of the evidence matching longitudinal psychometric evidence with brain morphology at autopsy was also an objective.

The Duke research team had proposed such a study for a number of years so that longitudinal evidence on cognitive functioning could be correlated with evidence of brain structure at death. Peer reviewers at the National Institutes of Health, however, were not convinced initially that such a study was feasible or that, given lack of consensus among scientists about the utility of research autopsies of the brain, such evidence would be useful.

At the end of data collection for the first study in 1976, NIH did authorize a special study to explore, first, the feasibility of managing the practical details of legal consent and securing the bodies for autopsy, and second, the research potential of brain autopsies in which neuropathologic findings could be related to longitudinal information on cognitive functioning.

The neuropathologic studies focused not only on general pathologic evaluation but also on quantification of neuronal populations and of senile plaque formation, neurofibrillary degeneration and granulovacuolar change. These findings could then be related to the longitudinal record of intellectual functioning of autopsied individuals as revealed by the previous 20 years of sequential psychologic testing.

The practical issues addressed in this special study are important for administrators of longitudinal research in which autopsy is included or proposed. When autopsy is proposed for a defined, institutional population whose death can be predicted and whose autopsy can be performed at the site of death, the only practical problem is to ensure legal permission to perform the autopsy. When, as in the case of the longitudinal panelists, identified persons who have agreed to the autopsy are likely to be geographically dispersed and for whom the time of and location at death are not determined, the logistical problems are more complex. For example, how does the scientific investigator maintain appropriate contact with the subject, the next-of-kin, and the probable attending physician so as to ensure notification of death? How does one ensure getting the body from the place of death to the site of autopsy in a timely way and return the remains to next-of-kin appropriately? These logistical problems are complex but solvable.

In regard to theoretical issues which might be clarified by autopsy, certain morphological changes that occur in a person with dementia in the pre- and post-senium have been consistently described. These changes include vascular disease with cerebral softening as well as the changes characteristic of senile dementia of the Alzheimer's type (SDAT): for example, senile plaques, neurofibrillary change, and granulovacuolar degeneration. In various studies it has been noted, however, that age-related alterations found in patients with SDAT are also present, although in more restricted locations and with less severe intensities, in nondemented individuals. Further, surveys of elderly patients sampled for pathologic study without selection for the presence or absence of dementia suggest that there appears to be a linear relationship between the number of senile plaques and decline in intellectual functioning in the six months prior to death.

The putative relationship between the intellectual change observed as in normative aging and the pathologic alterations which characterize SDAT is, therefore, of great interest. This critical relationship, however, has not been demonstrated definitively. An additional unresolved issue is the cortical neuronal depopulation, if any, associated with SDAT. Conflicting evidence has been published.

Methodology

Provision for Autopsy

Eight of ten surviving subjects from the First Longitudinal Study approached in 1976 agreed to autopsy with the concurrence of next-of-kin. The consent form which was signed both by the subject and by next-of-kin was approved by the Duke Medical Center Clinical

Investigations Committee and included the obligation of the Center to bear the cost of transporting the body within a distance of 100 miles and of cremation if the subject stated this preference. A procedure for regular communication between the Center and these special subjects was instituted. Nine years later, only four of these subjects have come to autopsy. The remaining subjects, in order to reinforce contact and to update information on psychological functioning, returned to the Center or were visited in their homes by a psychologist and a physician from the Center familiar to each subject.

Both family members and the physician of record are known to be aware of the desire of the identified older person to be autopsied. In the four cases autopsied, contact with the Duke Center has been initiated by family members at the time of death.

Neuropathologic Study

The procedure at autopsy is as follows. The brains of the deceased subjects are removed, weighed, and fixed in formalin. In a complete autopsy gross external examination requires attention to the state of the cerebral vessels, extent of cortical atrophy, and the presence of cerebral infarction. One coronal section is taken through the level of the optic chiasm and the extent of ventricular dilatation estimated.

The brain is then sent to Dr. Harold Brody at SUNY–Buffalo Medical School for studies in neuronal populations sampled from 15 areas of the cerebral hemispheres, the brain stem, and the cerebellum. The left cerebral hemisphere is then returned to Duke. At this point, comparable sections from areas to be studied by Dr. Brody are taken from 9 regions of the brain. Tissues are processed for routine paraffin embedded sections as well as frozen sections for the King silver stain to identify senile plaques and neurofibrillary tangles. After these sections are removed, the brain is cut into serial coronal sections. Evidence from the neuronal population study is not currently available.

Cortical atrophy is quantitated by the use of the black and white photograph of the specimens as noted above. The profile of the entire brain is cut out from this photograph and weighed. The darkened ("shadowed") areas of the sulci are then removed and similarly weighed. The weights form a ratio of sulci to total cross section of the brain to obtain an "atrophy index." A photograph of a characteristic coronal section is similarly weighed and compared to the weight of the profiles of the lateral ventricles. This produces a "lateral ventricular index" or percentage of the total cross-sectional area of the brain occupied by the lateral ventricles.

Routine microscopy is performed on hematoxylineosin Luxol-fast blue stains to evaluate the presence of general pathologic features such as cerebral infarction or for such specific age- and dementia-related findings as granulovacuolar degeneration in the hippocampus. The sections stained by the King method are reviewed for the presence of senile plaques and neurofibrillary tangles. For each of the sections, the number of these structures is quantitated in a grid with an area of 1.3 mm^2.

Findings

Profiles of Four Cases

Clinical and psychologic data obtained from the biomedical and psychological data of the First Longitudinal Study are combined with autopsy data in the brief characterization of cases which follow. The neuropathologic findings are summarized for the four available subjects in Table 3.6. WAIS profiles are summarized in Figures 3.1 to 3.4.

Case 1.   The patient was an 86-year-old female whose relatively stable Wechsler Adult Intelligence Scale (WAIS) scores are illustrated in Figure 3.1. The general autopsy defined the cause of death as emphysema and bronchopneumonia. The neuropathologic findings are summarized in Table 3.6. For Case 1, the brain weight of 1050 grams, 3 + cortical atrophy, an atrophy index of .20 and a ventricular index of .073 are noteworthy. Thirty-two percent of the superior cortical surface was occupied by sulci. An estimated 7.3% of the cross-sectional area of the brain at the level of the caudate nuclei was occupied by the lateral ventricles. Senile plaques were not seen in any of the sections except for a few lesions in the inferior frontal gyrus and amygdala. Neurofibrillary tangles were absent from the neocortex but were scattered within the glomerular formation of the hippocam-

Table 3.6. Summary of Pathology Findings at Autopsy for Four Cases

	Sex: Age:	Female, 86 years	Male, 94 years	Female, 87 years	Female, 88 years
Macroscopic					
Brain Weight		1050 grams	1230 grams	1150 grams	1201 grams
Atrophy		3+	1+	2+	2+
% Cortex Occupied by sulci		32	23	25	19
Microscopic					
Senile Plaques					
Middle Frontal		1	$22/mm^2$	$8/mm^2$	$0/mm^2$
Entorhinal Cortex		1	$11/mm^2$	$4/mm^2$	$0/mm^2$
Ammon's Horn					
$L_1 - L_5$ (Total number of plaques)		1	29	2	0
Neurofibrillary Change					
Middle Frontal		$0/mm^2$	$3/mm^2$	$0/mm^2$	$0/mm^2$
Entorhinal Cortex		$13/mm^2$	$10/mm^2$	$9/mm^2$	$3/mm^2$
Ammon's Horn					
$H_1 - H_5$ (Total number of tangles)		0	8	5	8

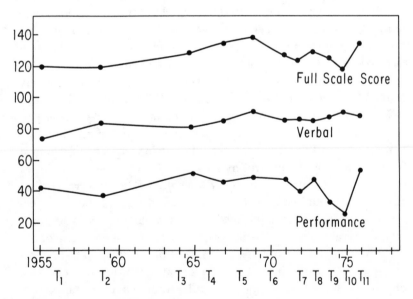

Figure 3.1. WAIS Profile: Case 1.

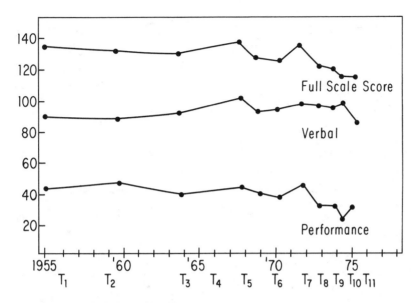

Figure 3.2. WAIS Profile: Case 2.

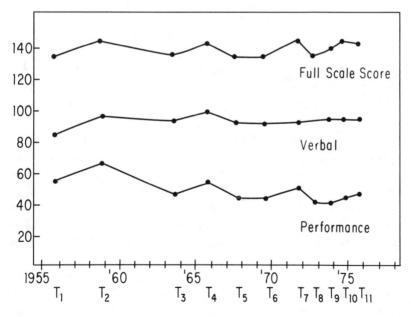

Figure 3.3. WAIS Profile: Case 3.

73

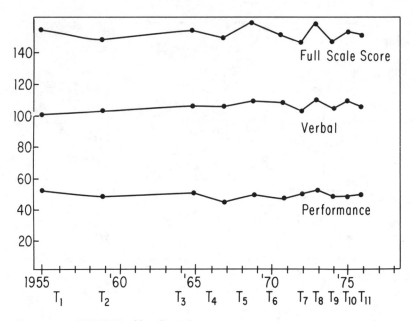

Figure 3.4. WAIS Profile: Case 4

pus. Granulovacuolar degeneration in the hippocampus was estimated at 2+. Hirano bodies were occasionally seen.

Case 2. Declining WAIS scores after the fifth time of measurement for this 94 year old male appear in Figure 3.2. The observed
decline in intellectual function occurred in the 4 years prior to death.
The intellectual deficit was so severe at the time of a special post-
study evaluation in 1979 that formal testing could not be done. The
immediate cause of death was acute bilateral bronchopneumonia.

On neuropathologic evaluation at autopsy (again see Table 3.6)
the brain weighed 1230 grams and illustrated a 1+ atrophy. The
atrophy index of the cerebral cortex was .18 and a similar index for
the ventricular size was .06. The percent sulcae area of the cerebral
cortex was 23 and a similar index of vertical size was 6. There were
many senile plaques and neurofibrillary tangles in all sections examined. The plaques ranged from 51 lesions in the precentral gyrus to
160 lesions in the inferior frontal gyrus. Neurofibrillary tangles were
present in all sections except the postcentral, superior temporal, and

cingulate gyri. They were most numerous in the hippocampus and amygdala where 35 such lesions were noted. Both granulovacuolar degeneration and Hirano bodies were present at a 2+ level.

Case 3. The overall WAIS performance of this 87 year old female was remarkably stable (see Figure 3.3). The neuropathologic findings are summarized in Table 3.6. The 1150 gram brain contained multiple cerebral infarcts, the largest in the right cerebral convexity. Severe atherosclerosis was present. There was only slight (2+) cerebral cortical atrophy. By a morphometric study, 25% of the cerebral cortical surface was occupied by sulci. The ventricles occupied 8% of the cross sectional area although the ventricles were asymmetrically enlarged as a result of the infarctions. A slight to moderate number of senile plaques ($8/mm^2$) were present in the frontal lobe and a less number ($4 mm^2$) were seen in the entorrhinal cortex. Only $1/mm^2$ were noted in Ammon's horn. Neurofibrillary change was not found in the frontal lobe. In the entorrhinal cortex, there were 9 tangles/mm^2. Ammon's horn contained a total of 5 tangles. A rare neuron in Ammon's horn contained granulovacuolar degeneration.

Case 4. The WAIS performance of this 88 year old female was notably stable over a period of two decades (Figure 3.4). With the single exception of the Digit Symbol Test subscore, WAIS subscores exhibited no decline.

The neuropathologic findings (Table 3.6) indicate moderate diffuse cortical atrophy. Evidence of hypertensive disease and old infarct was present in the right parietal; the cerebellum was unremarkable. A moderate number of neurofibrillary tangles were observed in Ammon's horn but senile plaques were not observed here nor in the cerebral cortex. Neurons with granulovacuolar degeneration were rare.

Significance of the Cases

Case 1. This subject's WAIS was essentially stable over a long period and only a few senile plaques and neurofibrillary tangles were seen at autopsy. The neuronal counts, yet to be completed, therefore, will provide information about the brain of an aged individual functioning cognitively in the normal range and without evidence of gross morphological pathology. The presence of cortical atrophy in this older individual is of interest because it suggests that cortical atrophy alone is not a correlate of dementia or cognitive dysfunction.

Case 2.   This subject illustrates the expected correlation between widespread senile plaque formation and neurofibrillary change with senile dementia of the Alzheimer's type (SDAT). Results of psychological testing define the character and duration of the intellectual decline about a decade prior to death. The cognitive and morphological findings quantify the relationships between the length and severity of the documented intellectual deficit and the numbers and topographic localization in the brain of senile plaques and neurofibrillary change. Neuronal counts for this subject when completed, therefore, will address the controversial question of whether there is or there is not neuronal depopulation in SDAT.

Cases 3 and 4.   These subjects illustrate alert, functional, stable individuals who succumbed to vascular disease. The high level and stability of their longitudinal WAIS scores correlate with the absence of significant pathological changes of SDAT.

4

The Aging Central Nervous System, Cognitive Functioning, and Behavior: Psychometric and Behavioral Findings

THE PROBLEM

The psychometric and behavioral research in the two longitudinal studies are complementary but different in both their emphases and their measurement procedures. In the first study, characterizing and understanding behavioral correlates in the aging central nervous system (CNS) were the primary objectives. The major psychological tests used were the Wechsler Adult Intelligence Scale (WAIS), (Wechsler, 1955); the Wechsler Memory Scale (WMS) (Wechsler, 1945); the Rorschach (1942) as a psychodynamic measure of the organization and integration of personality; and a specially designed reaction time task (CPT). Auditory functioning was measured with standard audiometric techniques.

The second study focused on and emphasized adaptive aspects of behavior. Assessments of psychological functioning were tied less to CNS functioning and oriented more to understanding the behavior of individuals in a social psychological framework. Data collected by the psychological laboratory included a shortened version of the WAIS, Cattell's 16 Personality Factors (16PF) Questionnaire (1962, 1970), standard audiometry, and an assessment of the individual's reaction time performance in a continuous performance task (CPT) with concomitant psychophysiological monitoring (Vigilance). All of the procedures for the administration, scoring, and data handling used in the psychological laboratory can be found in the Technician's Handbook (Siegler, Murray, Johnson & Rusin, 1976).

A detailed review of the major psychological issues addressed in both longitudinal studies and the theoretical and methodological backgrounds for these issues can be found in Siegler (1983). In addition to data collected by the psychological laboratory, other social psychological data were collected as a part of the social history of subjects (see Chapter Six).

Analysis of the psychological data was the responsibility of senior investigators of the psychology laboratory of the longitudinal studies. As in any large-scale study, the data that various investigators have chosen to emphasize reflected their own theoretical and methodological interests and sense of important issues in the psychology of aging.

It is important to place the two longitudinal studies in their appropriate sociohistorical contexts. The initial psychological data were collected for the first study in 1955 and for the second in 1968. The WAIS was a new test in 1955; and a developmental model for the psychology of aging was not introduced until Schaie's now classic paper appeared in *Psychological Bulletin* in 1965.

It is tempting to evaluate psychological research in longitudinal studies and the measures used on the basis of current information about alternative measurement procedures with the benefit of hindsight. At the time the two longitudinal studies were designed, however, the measures chosen were reasonable ones; only hindsight suggests that other instruments might have been more appropriate. In this chapter, highlights of findings from both longitudinal studies related to CNS function and psychological measurement of behavioral concomitants will be described. Then some critical comments will be made on the research methods used and implications for future research will be discussed.

PSYCHOMETRICS

Summary of Findings: The First Longitudinal Study

WAIS

Of the psychometric variables in the first study, the WAIS has been, expectedly, the most important because the study of adult intelligence is perhaps the best developed area within the psychology of adult development. A large number of papers published from the Duke studies have contributed to that development.

Data from the initial round examinations (1955–59) were used to evaluate the norms that had been published for the WAIS itself since norms for older persons were not developed as part of the original national standardization procedure. Instead, a special study was conducted in Kansas City (see Doplett & Wallace, 1955) to establish norms for older populations.

Eisdorfer and Cohen (1961) compared the Duke data with the data used for the proposed WAIS norms. They reported significant differences between their findings and proposed norms and recommended the development of standardized tables for older persons based on a national sample. A series of papers from the Duke longitudinal research team explored the potential of WAIS:

1. To specify the nature of intellectual functioning assessed cross-sectionally (Eisdorfer & Cohen, 1961) and assess intellectual performance longitudinally (Eisdorfer, 1963; Eisdorfer & Wilkie, 1974b);
2. To identify and illustrate methodological issues involved in evaluating changes in intelligence within a developmental model (Botwinick & Siegler, 1980);
3. To assess the impact of sample attrition on interpreting changes in intelligence in longitudinal research (Siegler & Botwinick, 1979); and
4. To study the relationship of intelligence to survival, distance from death and terminal drop (Wilkie & Eisdorfer, 1974; Siegler, 1975; Siegler, 1980).

In Botwinick's review (1977) of conclusions and interpretations based on published research on intellectual development during adulthood and old age, evidence from the Duke studies has made a notable contribution to the clarification of issues. The Duke data allow one to construct and compare alternative patterns of changes in verbal and performance intelligence with age, to illustrate longitudinally a high degree of stability in the later years in the absence of illness, and to assess the possible effects of cohort differences.

The WAIS as a measure of cognitive functioning in the Duke studies has been used productively in conjunction with other variables in the longitudinal data sets. These uses have clarified, for example, (1) the relationship between intellectual functioning and cardiovascular disease (Thompson, Eisdorfer & Estes, 1966; Siegler & Nowlin, 1979a); (2) blood pressure changes indicative of hypertension (Wilkie & Eisdorfer, 1971); (3) electrical activity (EEG) of the brain and cerebral blood flow (see Chapter Three above); (4) sleep EEG patterns (Prinz, 1977); (5) predictions of survival which included measures of longevity and social demographic indices (Palmore, 1974b; Pfeiffer, 1974); and (6) brain morphology at autopsy (see Chapter Three above).

The general conclusions about intellectual development in later adulthood reported by Duke investigators and replicated by others include (1) the maintenance of intellectual functioning as normative when assessed longitudinally, until about the 8th decade of life; (2) the superior maintenance of verbal as opposed to performance skills; (3) the negative impact of severe hypertension and cardiovascular disease on intellectual function, which suggests the importance of distinguishing reduced functioning due to disease rather than to normal aging; (4) the possible protective effect of mild levels of hypertension for intellectual functioning of older persons; (5) the strong relationship between levels of intellectual performance and subsequent survival; (6) the usefulness of distance from death as a variable in understanding changes with age in the terminal years of life; and (7) the usefulness of the WAIS as an important marker variable in understanding changes in the CNS as a function of normal aging.

Wechsler Memory Scale (WMS)

Parts of the Wechsler Memory Scale (WMS) were included in the first study in 1960 at the time of the second examination. Wilkie, Eisdorfer, and Nowlin (1976) investigated the impact of changes in memory functioning over a 6.5 year interval as a function of the individual's blood pressure. The results indicated that memory for verbal materials (stories and paired associates) was not related to changes in hypertension, but memory for figures was significantly impaired if hypertension had developed in the intervening years.

McCarty, Siegler, and Logue (1982) investigated the cross-sectional and longitudinal patterns of change observed in the memory. Cross-sectional patterns of WMS performance were evaluated with multiple regression. Age was related only to performance for immediate recall in logical memory and visual memory tasks; the age effects were linear, and negatively related to age. Educational attainment, rather than age, sex, or race, was the most important predictor of performance. For the longitudinal analyses, the subjects were divided into two cohorts, with average ages in the middle 60's for the younger cohort and the middle 70's for the older cohort. Longitudinally, consistent linear declines were found only for difficult paired associates and visual reproduction tasks.

Siegler, McCarty, and Logue (1982) also evaluated the effects of selective panel attrition on the WMS subtests on interpretations of intellectual change with age. Estimates of change in verbal memory (paired associates and logical memory) were found to be quite sensitive to attrition effects, especially for subjects in the older cohort. Visual memory as indexed by visual reproduction tasks was shown to be unaffected by attrition, suggesting that the declines in performance of panel survivors observed were more likely to be accurate reflections of the performance one would have observed had the entire sample survived to be tested.

Reaction Time (RT)

Wilkie, Eisdorfer, and Siegler (1975) compared the reaction time of longitudinal subjects with a matched group of younger persons. Results indicated that the older subjects were significantly slower in simple RT, choice RT, and RT following a conflict trial. Data from the older subjects over the next 3 examinations documented modest decremental changes. Siegler (1977b), evaluating RT changes over the first 5 examinations in the first study, found that mean changes in simple and complex reaction time were small. Cumulative frequency distributions developed for a subset of the subjects indicated that the major longitudinal change was in the increased variance of performance across time.

Siegler (1981) investigated choice RT performance averaged over 20 trials before the first conflict trial was introduced. Mean lift time (decision component), mean press time (visuo-motor component), and total RT were evaluated for a "young-old" (60–69) and "old-old" (70+) cohorts at the second through fifth times of measurement; analysis also included a second older group (the survivors of the young-old group who completed the 11 rounds of the first study).

There were no significant cohort/age differences between the young-old and older groups through the first four times of measurement; however, significant time effects were found for lift ($F=3.69$, $p<.013$) and press ($F=12.49$, $p<.001$) times. The lift times decreased significantly from approximately 505 msec. to 469 msec., while press times significantly increased from 360 msec. to 450 msec.; changes in total RT were non-significant. For the second older group, there were no significant differences for the press component, while both lift and total RT changed significantly in a non-linear fashion with the slowest RT's at the final measurement point. These results suggest that decrements in RT observed longitudinally may well be smaller than suggested by findings from traditional cross-sectional analyses.

Summary of Findings: The Second Longitudinal Study

Intellectual Function

The only psychometric data in the Second Longitudinal Study were derived from a modified WAIS. On the basis of experience in the first study, the parts of WAIS selected for use in the second study included Information and Vocabulary subtests to represent the verbal domain; and Picture Arrangement and Digit Symbol Substitution to represent the performance domain. These four subtests have been combined to estimate verbal, performance, and total scaled scores by arithmetic weighing.

Over the six years of the second study, intellectual functioning increased for the total sample through the third round of measurement and then stabilized. The initial average age of the panel was 55 years.

Intellectual Function and Health

Siegler and Nowlin (1979a) investigated the role of health status in relationship to changes in intellectual functioning. Individuals were selected from the second study panel who had a stable cardiovascular status over the six years of the study. *Normals* were those who had no disease initially and developed no disease; *hypertensives* were those classified clinically at the beginning and the end of the study.

The results indicated that *normals* and *hypertensives* who were receiving medication for this condition had the pattern described for the total sample: that is, they increased in intellectual function through the third measurement point. Subjects with coronary artery disease (CAD), or both CAD and untreated hypertension, had significantly lower mean levels of intellectual function initially and increased performance only through the second examination.

Other psychological studies conducted with data from the second study will be discussed below in the section on Behavioral Aspects of the Aging Person.

METHODOLOGICAL CONSIDERATIONS

None of the psychometric measures employed in the longitudinal studies was designed originally to be repeated measures. Parallel tests were not employed in the Duke studies nor were extensive substudies done with panelists to assess the practice effects that are certainly present in longitudinal studies. The practice effects suggested by data in the second study also appear to interact with age. The variance in the response of panelists is large. Thus, when the total sample and various sub-groups within the sample who, *a priori*, would be expected to respond differently to psychological tasks are compared, all show a particular trend which is interpretable as evidence of a practice effect.

Some limited studies performed in the Duke Center's psychological laboratory have evaluated practice effects in response to WAIS. In general, almost all subjects tend to gain in performance between first and second examinations even when the time between the two measurements is as much as four years. A special item analysis of 22 long-term subjects indicated, however, that practice effects were less apparent after the second examination.

While the longitudinal data may overestimate the level of maintenance of function because of the use of repeated measurements, decreasing distance from death may work in the opposite direction. Comparisons of the full-scaled WAIS scores of the Duke panels with published data from other samples suggest that most older subjects studied at Duke tend to be, on average, in the bright-average range.

The choice of the WAIS as a major instrument for psychometric studies of intelligence proved to have both advantages and disadvantages. The WAIS data allow for comparisons with other major longitudinal data sets of similar age (e.g., Riegel's Hamburg Data; the NIH Human Aging Study; Berkeley Growth Studies); however, WAIS data are not particularly useful in enhancing the understanding of the factorial nature of intelligence itself in relationship to models of adult intelligence such as the one proposed by Horn (1968, 1970). Special analysis in progress on the factorial nature of the WAIS (Siegler & Botwinick, 1980) suggests that 1) the 11 subjects of WAIS are essentially unifactor and a good representation of Spearman's "g" and 2) that a more differentiated factor structure appears only when race, sex, and education are added to the analysis.

The psychological profile of older adults that emerges from the psychometric data in the Duke Longitudinal Studies is essentially an optimistic one. The longitudinal changes in intelligence observed are relatively benign in late adulthood unless some disease process is present.

THE AGING PERSON:
BEHAVIORAL ASPECTS

This section addresses the measurement of personality, behavior, and auditory functioning from both longitudinal studies. The focus is on a set of social psychological constructs and a vigilance task included in the second study which emphasized behavioral rather than psychometric issues in the study of aging processes. Again, the different objectives and emphases of the two longitudinal studies should be noted.

The First Study

Personality was assessed by the Rorschach in the first study. Assessments were made at the first, second, and fourth round of examinations, spanning the first 10 years of the study. Eisdorfer (1960a&b, 1963) reported various findings from the Rorschach studies, concluding that (1) patterns of personality rigidity, often assumed to be the effect of aging, are more properly attributed to differences in intelligence; (2) visual impairments were not related to Rorschach performance among the aged; and (3) hearing impairment does have a significant negative impact on personality in the aged, particularly in terms of rigidity, functional integration, content, and index of primitive thought as assessed by the Rorschach. In addition to the work on the personality correlates of hearing impairment, Eisdorfer and Wilkie (1974a) also documented the normative longitudinal patterns of hearing loss.

The Second Study

For the second study, the major activity of the psychological laboratory shifted from a primary concern with psychometric issues to the collection of data that would provide dynamic assessments of behavior during middle and later life. The primary procedures used in the second study included Cattell's 16PF personality inventory; a short form of the WAIS (see section on psychometrics); standard audiometric testing; and a vigilance (CPT) task to assess reactions to stress.

Subjects were seen only for one day (in the first study three days of testing were required) and, in order to include the vigilance (CPT) task, time for other psychological testing was reduced. This explains the selection of four subtests of the WAIS, which could be administered in about half an hour, instead of the full WAIS. Form C of the 16PF was chosen because it is shorter and requires only an average reading level. Social history materials (see also Chapter Six) included many social psychological constructs related to self-concept and life events that are relevant to understanding behavioral aspects of aging processes.

Personality and Behavior

Siegler, George, and Okun (1979) evaluated the age/cohort and time effects observed in personality by employing a cross-sequential design with 12 two-year cohort groups. The results indicated that over the six-year study period of the second study personality tended to be stable. The most striking finding was the stability of personality indicators and of sex differences; the patterns varied neither by age/cohort nor by time. Five traits identified in 16PF displayed this stable profile: A (reserved vs. outgoing); E (submissive vs. dominant); I (toughminded vs. tenderminded); N (naive vs. shrewd); and Q4 (relaxed vs. tense). Females were found to be more outgoing, more submissive, more tender-minded, more naive, and more tense. Only one factor, B (a verbal intelligence, problem-solving factor) had significant time and age/cohort effects but not a sex effect. This finding for Factor B replicates other findings with the WAIS on this sample. Overall, some intellectual decline is evident.

There was a significant sex-by-time interaction for Factor O (guilt prone vs. confident); over time guilt proneness tended to decrease for males and to increase for females. A significant sex-by-cohort interaction for Factor Q1 (liberal vs. conservative thinking) was observed; in the oldest cohort males were more liberal but no difference was found in the youngest cohort.

Only on Factor O (guilt proneness) of 16PF do the data replicate the findings by Gutmann (1977) indicating a "unisex" trend in personality in later life.

George (1978) investigated the effect of personality and social demographic factors on life satisfaction and levels of social activity and involvement. Personality traits were significantly better predictors of life satisfaction than demographic factors. In contrast, demographic factors were better predictors of activity and social involvement than were personality traits.

Personality traits, the data suggest, are relatively stable during the middle years and are significantly related to other social psychological self-attributes. Whether the organization of personality is more subject to change in response to significant, particularly stressful, life experience rather than to aging *per se* warrants additional study.

The Continuous Performance ("Vigilance") Task (CPT)

A demanding and hence "stressful" laboratory task, the Continuous Performance Task (Harkins, Nowlin, Ramm & Schroeder, 1974), was incorporated into the second study protocol and behavioral, physiologic, and affective responses to the task were monitored. In the larger setting of a longitudinal study designed to evaluate the middle-aged and older person's adaptation to life stress, inclusion of a "stressful" laboratory procedure was particularly appropriate. Response to stress induced experimentally in a laboratory is an analog to and can be compared with responses to stressful life events. Also, even though the older individual has been evaluated frequently in stressful laboratory situations, the broad range of background information about panelists in the second Duke study was an advantage. For example, response to the "stress" of the Continuous Performance Task by panelists could be examined in relation to intelligence, health, and personality factors.

The CPT experiment included an initial session and a follow-up session four years later. At each session, the study protocol called for a single 10-minute or two 10-minute exposures to visual presentation of single-digit numbers at the rate of one number per second. Participants were instructed to press a key whenever they recognized a consecutive sequence of either two even numbers or two odd numbers. Precise order of number presentation closely followed that of Thompson, Opton, and Cohen (1963). Behavioral response variables included number of correct detections of number pairs, number of commission errors (i.e., inappropriate key response when odd or even numbers did not follow in sequence), and reaction time for correct responses. Two physiologic variables were recorded—heart rate and basal skin conductance. The Nowlis Mood Adjective Checklist (Nowlis, 1956), a quickly and easily performed pencil-and-paper assessment of mood, was employed to assess anxiety levels; this mood adjective checklist (MACL) was completed by the study participant before the first 10 minute CPT trial and before and after the second 10-minute CPT session.

Overall response accuracy (as reflected by number of correct detections and reaction time averaged over the four trials) was not found to be influenced by sex or age. Younger and older panelists in the second study were defined on the basis of those under and over the median panel age of 58. Overall number of commission errors, considered by some behavioral scientists to reflect willingness to take risks (e.g., Botwinick, 1966), was greater among the younger age group and among men.

Behavioral response between the two trials (averaged for the first session and second session four years later) demonstrated a decrease in both commission errors and reaction time. In fact, change in behavioral response over the four-year interval between CPT sessions (averaged over the two trials within each session) improved significantly. There was no between-session change in number of commission errors and neither sex nor age grouping influenced the pattern of behavioral change between trials or between the two sessions four years apart.

Physiological measures (heart rate and level of skin conductance), presumably indices of physiologic arousal, were quite responsive in the experimental setting. Each CPT trial was preceded by a 5-minute rest period when basal heart rate and skin conductance values were recorded. The format, then, provided pre-task and task values for both physiologic measures. Overall heart rate (averaged for the four pre-task and four task values) was not influenced by age grouping; overall value for skin conductance, however, was higher among the younger age group, a finding anticipated by earlier research in psychophysiology. Women presented higher overall levels of heart rate and lower levels of skin conductance than did men.

When compared to pre-task values, task-associated heart rate and skin conductance both increased. This pattern of task response in physiologic measures was apparent at both trials of the initial session as well as trials four years later. Comparison of the two physiologic measures at the initial and the later session demonstrated a between-session decrease in both overall heart rate and skin conductance. These time-related changes in physiologic response to the CPT task were not influenced by age or sex groupings.

Self-report of anxiety, as gauged by the Nowlis MACL, presented both age group and sex group differences. Older individuals in the panel indicated less anxiety than did younger ones, and men less than women, when scores were averaged over the MACL testings. Time-related effects were such that, in general, self-report of anxiety increased at each of the three testings on both the initial and the repeat testing four years later. However, the baseline of anxiety was, on average, lower at the second series of CPT tasks.

In summary, the CPT data suggest that, in response to a stressful laboratory situation, older adults retain their ability to adapt. Whether age-related strategies of adaptation are different and how they may differ warrant further study.

Life Events, Stress, and Adaptation

Growing older in a community setting exposes individuals to events and experiences that are potentially stressful and, hence, constitute natural experiments which test adaptative capacity. The second Duke study investigated five common life events and responses to them among panelists (Palmore et al., 1979). The five life events chosen were: (1) retirement of self; (2) retirement of spouse; (3) widowhood; (4) departure of the last child from the home; and (5) a major medical event defined by a hospitalization.

Individuals who experienced one or more of these events were compared with "no-event" controls (panelists who were at risk for the event but who did not experience it). A model of adaptation was developed which viewed adaptation as a process in which the response to the event would be likely to be influenced by physical, psychological, and social resources of the individual prior to and at the time of the event. This influence would be reflected both in the probability that the event would occur and in the observed response to the event.

The findings from longitudinal evidence prior to and following events, which will be discussed in greater detail in Chapter Six, indicated that resources (such as good health, intellectual capacity, adequate financial resources, and social support) were important in predicting both who experienced events and how they adapted to experienced events. The greater the available resources, the fewer the events that were experienced and the better the adaptive responses. Further, adequate adaptive capacity was generally demonstrated; and for most panelists, the life events studied produced few, if any, sustained negative outcomes.

Social History and the Experience of Aging

Most of the other behavioral studies in the second study were based on data from social history materials collected from panelists (see Chapter Six). These materials also provided an extensive data base for the examination of social psychological variables from the perspectives of both psychology and sociology.

Self-Concept, Retirement, Events, and Age-Identity

A series of dissertations of doctoral candidates in the Department of Sociology, including, for example, those by Breytspraak (1973), George (1975), Fox (1975), and Wilson (1980), have used this data base. The major topics and selected findings in these doctoral dissertations illustrate the importance of the social psychological evidence in the study for understanding adaptation in later life.

Breytspraak (1973), for example, examined discrepancies in "ideal" and "actual" self-concept, based on semantic differential rating scales. Results suggest that, as hypothesized, greater discrepancies in ideal/actual self-concepts are associated with symptoms of anxiety and the experience of negative affect in response to life events. In addition, discrepancies in ideal/actual self-concept are significantly related to demographic variables; greater discrepancies are also found among women, individuals of lower status, and those who have experienced age-related role loss.

George (1975) developed a model for predicting the transition from an age-identity as "middle aged" to a self-identity as "old." The results indicate that there are basically two subgroups of older persons. About 40% of the sample apparently used purely chronological age criteria in defining their age identity (i.e., age 65 is equated with being old). But about 60% of the sample defined age identity primarily in terms of age-related social and physical losses. Age-identity, therefore, is not a simple proxy for chronological age; age-identity as "old" is associated with both physical decline and social loss and the association remains when chronological age is controlled.

Fox (1975) examined the impact of retirement upon women in the second study. Her basic research design included a comparison of older women in the work force, older retired women, and older women who had been housewives throughout their adult lives. Her results indicated that psychological well-being was positively related to labor force participation; highest levels of positive affect and life satisfaction were observed among the working women and lowest levels were observed among lifelong housewives. Retired women were intermediate. Further, the greatest apparent cost of labor force participation among working women appeared to be a lower rate of community involvement. This factor was related to some decline in positive affect subsequent to retirement, although retired women retained over time a higher level of psychological well-being than the housewives (see also Fox, 1977).

Wilson's dissertation (1980) focused on the impact of life events upon health and psychological well-being during the middle and later years. Overall, the number of events experienced was relatively small and the effects were also relatively slight. Her work is of methodological as well as substantive significance. The results of her analyses suggest that the summing of life events (a common technique that presumably indexes the cumulation of stress) masks important differences in patterns of effects. In fact, various events have very different effects, not always negative. Therefore, the impact of specific life events on health and perceived well being should be examined separately.

The work of Kurt Back, a senior investigator of the longitudinal research team, and his associates has focused on issues of self, identity, and the meaning of self during later life. Their studies represent a valuable research contribution to the use of personal and biographical materials in understanding subjective experience of middle and later life. More specifically, they have developed a series of papers addressing:

1. Self-image and attitudes toward drugs (Brehm & Back, 1968; Back & Sullivan, 1978); "drug proneness" appeared to be a psychological set independent of age;
2. Self-image through the life span (Back & Gergen, 1968; Back, 1971; Back & Morris, 1974); the stability of imagery of self for individuals was pronounced;
3. Time and death metaphors (Back, 1974); among older persons, preferred metaphors are quite varied; and
4. Life graphs as a tool for understanding continuity and change across the life span (Back & Bourque, 1970; Bourque & Back, 1969, 1977); older individuals have distinctly personal views of the best and worst periods of their life course development.

A Special Behavioral Study:
Perception of Stress
and Response Strategies

Panelists of the longitudinal studies were used for several related but more restricted ancillary investigations. In one study (Siegler, Gatz, Tyler & George, 1979; George & Siegler, 1981), 100 subjects from the second study were interviewed for a 5th time. The purposes of the study were 1) to investigate, through in-depth interviews, the individual's perception of stressful and related coping skills and strategies and 2) to develop a typology of life events in terms of the meaning of the events to those who experienced them. Information about the subjects' own views of, explanations for, and perceptions of the significant events in their lives was used to construct personal accounts of life events.

The findings suggest that older adults are very clever and resourceful in developing strategies to cope with events in their lives. Moreover, personal accounts of life events and their significance do not match prevailing assumptions about their significance. Events involving personal loss that are experienced and events that are considered important are not synonymous. Distinctly individual differences in assessing the personal meaning of events were evident as were differences in strategies of response that stressed, variously, seeking information, denial, and active confrontation of the perceived source of stress. This study is an example of an appropriate use of a longitudinal panel for satellite studies to explore personal variations in the experience of aging processes.

COMMENTS ON METHODOLOGY IN BEHAVIORAL PSYCHOLOGY

The following points are emphasized regarding the methodology of behavioral research in aging because they constitute important recommendations for future research:

While the second study was designed to be sensitive to cohort differences (five-year age cohorts were used typically), the measurement interval of two years and the lack of replacement samples of new members of the cohorts at later years makes it difficult to use the classical types of data analysis. Additional attention to the implications of how cohorts are defined and how study samples are maintained is needed because these problems affect the interpretation of findings.

Many of the social psychological measures used initially in the Duke studies because they were commonly reported in published literature on aging and could be used for comparison were known to have only moderate reliability (coefficients of 0.5 and 0.6). The choices reflected the state-of-the-art over the past two decades of gerontological research. This moderate level of reliability inevitably makes the separation of "true" change difficult to discriminate from unreliability of measures.

Many of the measures used were shortened forms of original instruments (e.g., an 11-item Locus of Control instrument; 7-item semantic differential instrument; Form C of Cattell). While these decisions by the Duke research team were defensible in order to include a larger range of variables within the limited examination time per subject of the Duke studies, exact replication of traditional instruments with higher reliabilities would have made the data easier to compare with findings with other research reported in the literature. This problem represents a persistent dilemma in large-scale multidisciplinary, longitudinal research.

In the specification of life events experienced by panelists, data were collected in such a way that the occurrence of an event between visits could be documented. Locating occurrence precisely in time was more difficult. The usefulness of data about life events to study the impact of these events is enhanced by the exact temporal specification of their occurrence in relation to each other and to the social and personal context in which they occur. This is difficult to achieve when the measurement interval in a longitudinal study is one or two years.

As in any multipurpose, multidisciplinary study, compromises inevitably are made in the interest of including a broad range of data that address the interests of different disciplines. The rich set of data of the Duke studies that can be used to investigate many broad issues are, however, not always adequate for focused, single-discipline studies that require extensive data on a smaller range of variables. In multidisciplinary longitudinal research, the trade-off of focus and precision against breadth of coverage presents a persistent dilemma. In compensation for sacrifice of focused inquiry, both Duke longitudinal data sets are particularly well-suited to answer questions that cut across disciplinary boundaries. The relationships of health and behavior as both change over time have been and will continue to be a major contribution of the Duke Longitudinal Studies.

The overall stability of personality, the observed sex differences, and the responsiveness of social psychological indicators to life events have been major findings of the Duke studies. These findings suggest that, in understanding adult development as a normal process, the models and theories advanced to understand adult development over the entire life course are applicable to older adults. Chronological age by itself accounts for very little of the variance observed in behavior. Developing models of coping, of adaptation, and of responses to significant life events that take into consideration stability as well as change over the life course is essential for understanding important aspects of behavior in the middle and later years.

5

Experimental Evidence from Ancillary Studies on Cognitive Changes with Age and Their Psychophysiological Correlates

Two major objectives guided these experimental research studies which complemented the Duke Longitudinal Studies. The first was to determine whether the ability to process nonverbal information undergoes a greater decline with age than does the ability to process verbal information. The second was to investigate the relation of this differential cognitive decline (if present) to the functional asymmetry of the cerebral hemispheres. These objectives bear directly on a central issue in the psychology of aging: Do all mental operations decline equally with advancing age, or is the decrement limited to only selected operations?

These ancillary experimental studies used subjects and procedures which were not routinely included in the two longitudinal studies. Specific attention must be given, therefore, to providing briefly essential methodological details for each experiment.

EXPERIMENTS IN COGNITION: METHODS AND FINDINGS

Verbal and Nonverbal Representation

The results of psychometric testing over the lifespan have repeatedly shown that scores on verbal tasks remain fairly stable, while scores on visuo-spatial tasks decline substantially (Botwinick, 1977). Elias and Kinsbourne (1974) carried out a memory study that controlled many of the extraneous factors which contribute to psychometric test results. Their data partially supported the hypothesis of a disproportionate decline in spatial skills. A related and important observation is that young adults frequently report using visual images to aid their memory for verbal information, whereas the elderly rarely do so (Craik, 1977).

The proposed experiments sought to extend these findings using a variety of memory paradigms, especially those measuring reaction time (RT). Memory is an important cognitive function to study in this context, since information can be coded in memory in a variety of ways (e.g., visual, phonemic, semantic), and RT paradigms can be employed to measure the formation and use of these coding processes (Posner, 1978). In addition, there is considerable evidence that in humans these coding processes are differentially represented in the left and right cerebral hemispheres (Moscovitch, 1979).

There are a number of possible reasons for a disproportionate decline in spatial skills over age. For example, many mental operations appear to slow with advancing age. If the elderly take excessively long to generate nonverbal representations, the usefulness of such representations (e.g., as a visual image) would be reduced.

Coding Verbal Information

In one experiment the time young and older adults required to "recode" verbal information into a more visual or spatial form was measured. This experiment employed the paradigm of Seymour (1974), who found that when a word and a shape (e.g., "square" and □) are visually presented at the same time, young adults are slower at responding "same" than when two shapes are presented.

However, when the shape follows the word by one second, "same" RT decreases to the level of the two-shape condition. It thus appears that younger subjects recode the word into some form of visual representation during the one second inter-stimulus interval. If the elderly are slow in forming such representations, then their response latency to a word-shape pair should remain longer than latency to a pair of shapes across the inter-stimulus interval.

In an experiment using this method, however, Nebes (1976) found that the RT pattern was quite similar for young and older adults. For both age groups, word-shape RT significantly decreased across the inter-stimulus interval (see Figure 5.1). The speed with

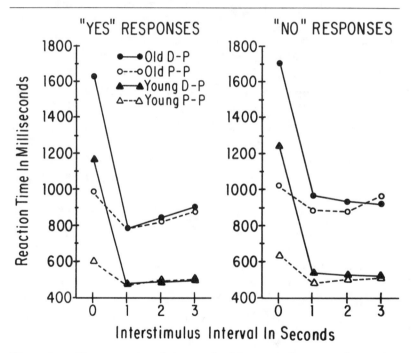

Figure 5.1. Response time by age of subject as a function of stimulus material. "Yes" and "no" response time for young and old subjects, as a function of stimulus material and interstimulus interval, in the Nebes (1976) experiment. In the D-P (description-picture) condition a word and shape were presented; in the P-P (picture-picture) condition two shapes were presented.

which verbal information can be recoded into a more visual form does not appear to change with age.

Although performing the verbal-pictorial recoding task requires the use of some form of visual information, the task does not necessarily require the use of visual images. In another experiment Nebes and Andrews-Kulis (1976) employed a task that encouraged subjects to use visual images. Subjects were given pairs of nouns and asked either to produce a sentence including the two words or to generate a mental image incorporating the two referents of the nouns. The time between the presentation of the words and the subject's report of the sentence or image was measured. No significant age difference in the time required to form either sentences or images was found. One aspect of the results, however, suggested older subjects were in fact not forming images. For the young subjects, the time required to form an image was affected by the rated "visualizability" of the words, but this was not true for the elderly subjects. It is thus possible that this method was not successful in measuring the elderly subjects' image formation time.

Another study (Nebes & Elias, 1978) followed up the findings of Nebes (1976) by investigating how rapidly young and older adults could recode information in the opposite direction—from a visual to a verbal form. Subjects were shown novel random shapes and asked to produce a name or verbal description for each one. Young individuals often report doing this spontaneously to aid their memory for visual material. Again, however, no effect of age on RT was evident in this stimulus recoding.

Following the labelling task, a surprise recognition test was given for the shapes that did reveal the expected age decrement in visual memory. The results of this study suggest that any visual memory deficit that does appear in the elderly cannot be attributed to a failure to encode the stimulus rapidly into a verbal representation.

Memory and Recall

The next study (Schear & Nebes, 1980) concentrated on memory for verbal and spatial information when recoding was not involved. Recall of the verbal and spatial aspects of the same stimulus array was required under identical stimulus conditions. Subjects were shown seven letters in a 5×5 grid and asked to recall either the letter names or their positions in the grid. The results indicated that while the elderly performed significantly worse than the young overall, there was no evidence that there was a disproportionate decline in their memory for the spatial characteristics of the stimulus array. However, evidence was not conclusive that the older subjects were actually using a spatial form of memory to remember the letter positions. Given the demonstrated ability of older individuals to recode spatial information into a verbal description, they may have used a verbal code for both letter name and letter position.

Rate of Processing

Previous work has shown that elderly individuals are substantially slower than the young on almost every task studied, and our own results confirm this. Consequently, it has been frequently suggested that there is a basic age-related change in the speed with which the central nervous system operates and that all mental operations are consequently carried out more slowly in the aged brain. If this proposition is correct, then age differences in speed of performance should exist regardless of the specific conditions of the task. Control conditions associated with the recoding paradigm of Nebes (1976) suggest the contrary.

Response Time and Age

Nebes demonstrated that the nature of the motor response determined whether or not an age difference in RT is observed. When subjects were required only to make a sound to the onset of a visual cue (simple vocal RT), no age difference in response speed was evident. This result was replicated and extended in a formal experiment (Nebes, 1978).

In a simple RT task, the typical age difference in speed was found when subjects were required to make a manual response. When the task required a vocal response (i.e., a sound), however, then the elderly subjects were not significantly slower than the young. These results argue against the existence of a general age-related slowing of all information processing operations and suggest, instead, that the slowing may be restricted to some but not all neural systems.

It is difficult to reconcile these findings with recent theories explaining age differences in RT in terms of age-related differences in health, arousal, or physical fitness. The present results demonstrate that within the same individuals, simple RT is determined by whether the required response is vocal or manual.

Complexity of Comparison

Although these findings argue against a general slowing-with-age hypothesis, age differences in RT are probably not completely determined by the nature of the response. It is likely that the number and/or complexity of the cognitive operations required for a decision is also an important factor; this is suggested, for example, in an investigation of hybrid memory-search/visual-search tasks in which subjects must compare a set of items (letters) held in memory against those presented in a visual display of two letters (Madden & Nebes, 1980a). The size of the memory set was either one, two, or three letters. In this task, the *rate* of comparison is reflected in the degree to which decision RT increases with the number of comparisons required for a decision. In this experiment, the search was significantly slower for the older than for younger subjects as indicated by the fact that age differences in decision RT increased as the number of items in the memory set was increased from one to three. Both age groups, however, were able to improve substantially their performance during extensive practice with the same memory-set items.

Some evidence indicated that the number of cognitive operations was also influential in determining age differences in nonverbal processing. For example, it can be seen in Figure 5.1 (above) that, in the verbal-pictorial recoding paradigm, the age difference in RT at the 0 sec interval is 80 msec larger in the word-shape condition (where recoding is required) than in the two-shape condition. A more direct estimate of the rate of nonverbal processing was obtained by Gaylord and Marsh (1975), who measured the time subjects required to determine whether two visually presented shapes were identical or were mirror images (see Figure 5.2). This task is often called "mental rotation," since subjects report that they rotate an image of one figure in an attempt to make it congruent with the other. The typical find-

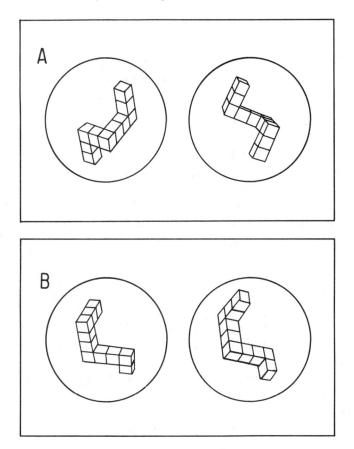

Figure 5.2. Illustration of stimulus material. These two panels illustrate by example what the subject saw on single trial. **A**. The subject saw these two stimuli in this configuration. The stimulus on the right is the same as the line figure on the left rotated by 140 degrees. **B**. A mirror image pair which cannot be rotated into congruence.

ing is that decision RT increases with the degree of orientation by which the two figures differ.

When both young and older adults were tested in this task, age differences in RT did increase with the different degree of orientation distinguishing the figures. The older subjects' RT increased more rapidly than that of the young as degree of orientation varied to make the operation more difficult. In fact, the proportion by which the rate of mental rotation was slowed for the older subjects was quite similar in magnitude to the age-related slowing in the rate of search reported by Madden and Nebes (1980a).

Cerebral Lateralization

Whether measurable changes in hemispheric function occur with age and are associated with corresponding changes in cognitive ability was also investigated. One method for measuring hemispheric function is tachistoscopic presentation to the left and right visual fields. The visual pathways are arranged so that information presented to the right visual field is first processed by the left cerebral hemisphere, whereas left visual field information is processed initially by the right cerebral hemisphere. By presenting information selectively to each visual field, at a duration too brief to permit eye movements (i.e., tachistoscopically), evidence regarding the processing abilities of each cerebral hemisphere can be obtained (Madden & Nebes, 1980b). In right-handed individuals, decisions regarding verbal items are typically made more rapidly and accurately as a result of right visual field (left hemisphere) presentation than as a result of left visual field (right hemisphere) presentation. There are some tasks involving visual coding that are more efficiently performed with stimuli presented to the left visual field (right hemisphere).

Processing Words and Pictures

In an initial study of visual field differences (Nebes, Madden & Berg, 1981) vocal RT for words and pictures was measured. On each trial, subjects named as rapidly as possible either a word or a picture that was presented to either the left or the right visual field. As expected on the basis of previous work, young subjects were faster in naming words presented to the right visual field (left hemisphere) than those presented to the left visual field (right hemisphere). If, as previous psychometric research findings suggest, right hemisphere functions are more disrupted by age than are left hemisphere functions, then the size of difference in vocal RT by visual field should be increased in the elderly subjects.

The results, however, indicated that the visual field difference was of equal magnitude in the two age groups. A dichotic listening test performed with these same subjects also yielded a left hemisphere (right ear) advantage in reporting verbal stimuli that was constant across age.

One limitation of this study was that an expected left visual field (right hemisphere) advantage for naming pictures was not evident in either age group. It could thus be claimed that right hemisphere functions were not directly tested. A second experiment (Nebes et al., 1981) attempted to elicit right hemisphere processing by including a condition in which the stimuli were visually presented clock faces. The time required for subjects to name the hour indicated by the clock face was in fact significantly faster for left visual field (right hemisphere) presentation than for right visual field (left hemisphere) presentation. The magnitude of this right hemisphere advantage, however, was equivalent for the young and elderly subjects. In none of these studies, therefore, has the evidence obtained demonstrated decline in the functional efficiency of one cerebral hemisphere with age more than the other.

Conclusions from Cognitive Experiments

These experimental studies did not support the dominant hypothesis in psychometric research in aging that nonverbal information processing undergoes a greater decline with age than does verbal processing. Although older adults frequently report that they rarely choose to employ visual mediators in memory tasks, this is apparently not because they are unable to do so. Demonstrably, they can generate both visual and verbal mediators and can do so as rapidly as younger adults.

A significant age-related increase in RT did appear in these experimental studies. The magnitude of this increase appears to be determined by both the complexity of the decision and the nature of the response required. The proportion by which the rate of cognitive processing slowed over age was similar for verbal and nonverbal processes. Finally, experiments measuring visual field differences in stimulus identification yielded no evidence suggesting that the right and left cerebral hemispheres are differentially affected by advancing age.

PSYCHOPHYSIOLOGICAL
CORRELATES OF COGNITION

Experimental studies to explore psychophysiological correlates of cognitive processes were conducted to identify ways in which the age-related physiological changes are associated with cognitive processes. The objective of the studies reviewed here was two-fold: (1) to establish ways in which specific physiological changes with age affect the way in which the mind functions, and (2) to test current psychological models of how the mind processes information using both physiological and behavioral data.

During the past decade several aspects of the electrophysiology of the brain have been shown to affect cognitive functioning. A case in point is research on physiological correlates of "event-related" potential (ERP) extracted from the EEG studies of brain functioning. Selected components of the ERP have been hypothesized to index levels of arousal and the timing of specific aspects of information processing during cognitive tasks (Molfese, 1980; Pritchard, 1981). Such indices can be used to measure changes in these functions with age. Behavioral measures such as reaction time (RT) can also be used to enhance interpretations of ERP data.

Since changes in cognition in later life can have many causes, ranging from disease processes to complications from drug therapies to normal aging processes, experiments are useful in distinguishing normative changes inherent in normal aging from secondary processes related to disease or to the medical management of illness.

Memory Search Tasks

A great deal of interest in psychophysiological research has centered on eliciting conditions for a component of the ERP variously labelled P_{300}, P_3 or "late positive component" (LPC). Figure 5.3 provides an example. The amplitude (size) of this component is measured from a baseline approximately at the point where N_{100} declines to P_{300}. LPC increases when it is elicited by a rare event, especially when the event is a target for which the subject is searching among other stimuli. The latency of the LPC is thought to mark the completion

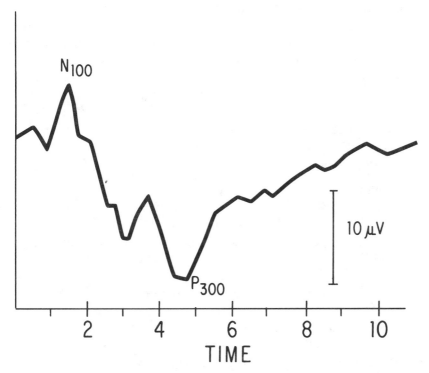

Figure 5.3. Example of ERP Record. An example of an ERP recorded from
the parietal scalp (P_z) with the components N_{100} and P_{300} noted.
The average was derived from 45 flashes of a dim light about
which the subject had to make brightness judgments. The time
is given in tenths of seconds and the vertical bar shows the size
of 10 microvolts for comparison to the ERP.

of the processes involved in evaluating a stimulus (Kutas, McCarthy
& Donchin, 1977).

Since the details of this process are, at best, vaguely understood,
a very simple memory search task was used to test the hypothesis
that the evaluation process in cognition is age related; older adults
take longer to reach a conclusion than younger adults.

The model chosen for the experiment was that of Sternberg
(1969) in which a subject is given a short list of digits to hold in
memory followed by a single "probe" digit. The subject responds

as to whether or not this probe digit is one of the set of numbers being held in memory. It is well established that the longer the list of numbers being held in memory (the set size), the longer the decision time. In a young adult population the time taken to "scan" mentally digits in memory has been shown to take about 40 msec per digit. If the LPC is emitted at the end of the scanning process as hypothesized, then longer lists should give rise to later LPCs in a calculatable fashion.

LPC Latency

In the experiment LPC latency did increase as length of lists increased (Marsh, 1975, 1976). This was true for both young and older adults. The average increase in latency time in the younger subjects was 12 msec. per digit; and for the older subjects, 22 msec. While this difference is large, it is only on the borderline of statistical significance.

This question was investigated again (Watson, 1977) with some improvements in procedures. Instead of two groups, older and younger subjects in the new experiment were selected from across the range of adult ages (20–65). It was, therefore, possible to observe LPC latency change over a broader range of ages.

This experiment, like the earlier one, however, did not find an age-by-set size interaction with LPC latency. The larger set sizes did not produce longer LPC latencies in the older subjects than in the younger. The LPC amplitude did exhibit such an interaction with older subjects having smaller LPC amplitudes on average. Moreover, since the LPC evidence was obtained from data averaged over trials, a greater variability of individual LPCs from trial to trial, when averaged, could lead to a broader, lower amplitude LPC. Thus, the implication is that memory search is slower for older than for younger subjects.

An interesting incidental result of this experiment was that the largest age effects for the ERPs were found at locations T_5 and T_6 (which are locations several centimeters behind each ear) rather than at the more traditional locations of F_z, C_z, and P_z. Further, in an analysis of data from the posterior temporal region, younger subjects exhibited an asymmetry in that the LPC and N_{100} were larger at the right temporal site. The older subjects did not show this asymmetry but did have a longer LPC latency in the right posterior temporal region which was not found in the younger subjects. The ERP data from the parietal scalp (P_z) were the basis of the comparisons reported above in order to correspond more closely to reports in the existing literature.

In summary, the LPC grew smaller as memory set size was increased; and this effect was larger for the older than for younger adults. The LPC was also larger for the response "match" than it was for "nonmatch."

Attention Studies

The same set of experiments was used to test several other propositions about changes in cognitive abilities with age. Older adults have been shown to have difficulty in ignoring irrelevant stimuli (Rabbitt, 1965). Two experiments tested the extent to which extraneous, interfering information hampers information processing.

One experiment used the Sternberg procedure (described above) with flanking digits appearing on both sides of the probe digit on some of the trials. Half of the flanking digits were from the same set as the probe. The other half were from the opposite set. For example, if the list of digits was 5 2 9 1 and the probe digit was 2, then an experimental set of 9 2 9 should lead to the same response, *match*. However, if the flanking digits in a set were 6s, as 6 2 6, the response would be *nonmatch*.

The flanking digits, especially in the conflict situation, did lead to slower reaction times by both young and old subjects. However, both old and young were equally affected.

A parallel experiment used a simple assignment scheme in which response to two sets of three digits was assigned to each hand. If any of the three digits assigned to the left hand appeared, then a "left hand" keypress response was appropriate. If a digit assigned to the right hand appeared, then a right hand response was called for. The probe digit appeared under three conditions: no flankers, flankers at 0.5 degrees of visual angle, and flankers at 2 degrees of visual angle.

The results were very similar to the findings of the previous experiment. A judgment and response based on a simple memory search and a judgment based on matching give the same results; older subjects did not take longer to sort out the probe digits from the flanking digits. This contradicts the usual conclusion found in the literature on interference. However, it should be noted the oldest subject in the two experiments reported was only 65 years of age and hence too young to exhibit the slower responses usually associated with very old adults.

Effects of Interference

Effects of interference on cognitive processes were explored further with the method first described by Stroop (1935). In this method, the subject is shown names of colors. The name of the color can be spelled in ink of the same color or in ink of a different color (the conflict situation). When the color name and the ink color are different, subjects tend to take longer to name the color of the ink. The same result can be obtained if the subject presses one or more keys to indicate the color of the ink. Several explanations of this result have been offered. One is that access to the physical stimulus and name codes in memory are both carried out automatically, and in parallel, during the early stages of cognitive processing. The meanings of the stimulus precede a "response" stage in which possible conflict must be resolved. The resolution of this conflict is expected to increase RT in the conflict situation (Posner & Snyder, 1975). A second explanation has been proposed (Hock & Egeth, 1970) based on the notion that perceptual encoding is speeded when the stimulus meanings are congruent and slowed when the meanings are in conflict. An experiment was designed to test whether changing the cognitive task could alter the subject's attention strategy in such a fashion that the Stroop effect would be greatly diminished as suggested by Treisman (1969). A second objective of the experiment was to assess whether one hemisphere would be more likely to respond to word meaning and the other to color. Thus, stimuli were presented selectively to either the left or right hemisphere on a given trial.

Comparison of responses to *word meaning* and responses to *color of the stimulus* produced several significant results (Warren & Marsh, 1978, 1979). Faster responses from the left hemisphere were observed to the meaning of the word. A strong Stroop effect indicated by longer RTs was observed in conflict conditions (see Table 5.1). No interactions of conditions with hemisphere were found. Thus, the results are consistent with the hypothesis that older subjects can attend to a stimulus dimension (rather than target values) and that automatic processing of both physical and name codes occurs.

The ERP elicited by the stimuli in the experiment showed no difference between "same" and "conflict" stimuli when the subject focused on the physical color. However, when the subjects focused on word meaning a negative component (N_{100}) was enhanced for the "same" condition. There were no differences, however, in amplitude or latency for the LPC. With regard to hemispheric asym-

Table 5.1. Mean Reaction Time (in Milliseconds) to Same (S) and Conflict (C) Stimuli, as a Function of Instrumental Condition and Visual Field of Presentation

Right Field (Left Hemisphere)		
Condition	S	C
Color	442	462
Word	473	384
Memory Color	491	538
Memory Word	538	549

Left Field (Right Hemisphere)		
Condition	S	C
Color	452	478
Word	478	492
Memory Color	536	532
Memory Word	531	562

metry of processing, the general result was that the N_{100} exhibited a shorter latency in the hemisphere receiving direct input; and the effect was greater for the color condition than for the word meaning condition.

In a second part of this experiment, subjects responded by matching the preceding stimulus to one that followed on the basis of physical color or word meaning. A robust Stroop effect was observed; preferential access to word codes in the left hemisphere and color codes in the right hemisphere was also observed.

When attention is directed to a particular aspect of a stimulus, the expected interference from automatic processing of irrelevant stimulus features can be avoided. However, avoidance of interference occurs only when stimulus processing is initiated in the preferred hemisphere for that feature. For instance, color tends to be processed with least interference from word meaning in the right hemisphere. Thus, the general position of Posner and Snyder (1975) is supported. ERPs were not analyzed for this set of experimental conditions.

Drugs and Memory

One of the major complaints of older adults is that memory becomes less functional with age. Since the neurotransmitter acetylcholine has been shown to be involved with memory function and has also been shown to be reduced as a person grows older, the capacity of an acetylcholine precursor to improve memory or other related cognitive performance of older adults was studied. A group of subjects with moderately deteriorated cognitive performances was selected from panelists in the First Longitudinal Study (Marsh & Linnoila, 1979). The drug Deanol, a precursor to acetylcholine, was chosen for testing as a potential enhancer of memory function because its use had been reported to improve memory function in hospitalized elderly patients.

The drug was given daily over a period of four weeks with testing at weekly intervals to detect drug effects on task performance. A battery of tests was employed to test cognitive functions. The study was double blind with half of the subjects receiving a placebo.

No improvement on any of the cognitive tests was shown by subjects receiving the drug. However, ERPs were enhanced in amplitude for subjects receiving the drug in several of the tests. No ready explanation of this dissociation between lack of behavior response in spite of a physiological response is available at this time although the anomaly has also been reported in animals.

Another issue addressed by these experiments was first raised by Rabbitt (1964), who demonstrated that a warning stimulus could speed performance in the young but was not similarly helpful to older subjects. However, when the warning stimulus gave incorrect information, performance was slowed in both groups; the older subjects clearly were not ignoring the warning information.

In the drug experiment older subjects were able to use warning information to speed their responses, both with and without the drug. The most likely explanation for the difference between the results of this experiment and those of Rabbitt earlier is that the current task was simpler. Rabbitt had forced subjects to respond according to moderately complicated rules that had to be thought through on each trial in order to respond properly.

Habituation

Early reports of age-related changes in evoked potential responsivity (Schenkenberg, 1970; Beck, Dustman & Schenkenberg, 1975) had shown that the later (e.g., 100 msec.) components of response were of lower amplitude in older age groups. Further, the reported reduction in amplitude of later components of response started as early as 40 years of age and became more pronounced with age.

The experiment was simple. Subjects had only to remain quiet during the recording of evoked potential or, at most, if the stimulus was visual, to keep eyes open. The objective of the experiment was to clarify whether the reduction in amplitude observed in a passive stimulation condition could be due to more rapid habituation by older subjects.

The hypothesis that habituation effects are different under conditions of passive and active stimulation was tested as follows. The first two large components of the visual evoked potential (N_{100} and

P_{200}) were measured under two different sets of instructions to subjects. First, the subject merely watched flashes of light on a screen. Second, the subject actively judged each flash of light to determine if it was slightly less intense than the other stimuli (2 of 20 were slightly dim). No statistically significant differences were seen in the components measured of EP from F_z, C_z, or P_z under the two conditions. Thus, this study does not indicate that more rapid habituation to stimuli occurs in older subjects.

Auditory Change with Age

A number of experiments were designed in the psychophysiology laboratory to increase understanding of the ways in which the auditory system changes with age. Some of the studies examined receptor and lower level auditory functions while others focused on the higher levels of the central nervous system. The latter studies were mainly concerned with how the ability to comprehend speech decreases with age.

Lower Level Auditory Functions

The studies of lower level auditory functions focused on ways in which signals might be altered by the ear (Hall, 1977, 1979). Narrow-band white noise masked pure tone signals not only within the noise band but also for all frequencies above the noise band. The masking effect for frequencies above the masking noise is much more powerful for older adults than for younger persons. The auditory system of an older person would be more likely to distort these complex signals since the older ear is less able to reproduce higher frequencies.

The ability of the auditory system to process pure tone signals was measured by recording "frequency following" (Smith, Marsh, Greenberg & Brown, 1978) in the evoked potentials from the brainstem (Hall, 1979). The EP responses recorded from the brainstem reflected the waveform of the stimulus but did not represent accurately residual pitch, another aspect of the stimulus that could be important in auditory function of older persons. *Residual pitch* is a low pitch generated by the auditory system when two or more harmonic pitches are present (Hall & Soderquist, 1978). Low pitch sounds that are not present in the physical stimulus are "heard" because several harmonics of that low pitch are present in the sound (e.g., one might hear 400 Hz simply because 800, 1200, and 1600 Hz are present).

Implications for Understanding Speech

The relevance of this observation for speech perception is that most older persons have greatly elevated thresholds for sounds about 4000 Hz, and the loss of hearing in these higher pitches could possibly reduce the ability of the older person to "generate" the lower residual pitches. Speech normally generates many frequencies in the range above 4000 Hz and they are crucial to understanding the spoken words. It seems possible that older adults are progressively unable to use high frequency auditory stimuli to generate some of the normal low frequencies that the central nervous system uses to process speech.

Other factors contribute to the difficulty in understanding speech experienced by many older people. Difficulty in screening out irrelevant information is one such factor. One experiment investigated the ability of older persons to locate the point in space from which a sound emanated (Herman, Warren & Wagener, 1977) since screening out irrelevant sounds is facilitated by pinpointing the location of the sound to which one wishes to attend.

Subjects were seated in a dimly lighted, acoustically damped room. The sound (a moderate intensity short tone) was delivered through earphones. At equal intensity and simultaneously delivered to both ears, short tones sound as if they are located in the center of the head. Differences in time of delivery or in intensity to one or the other ear creates the sensation of a tone to the left or right of the center of the head. The task for subjects was to press a key whenever the sound was detected to have moved away from the center. Older subjects required deviations of approximately twice the magnitude required by younger subjects before they could detect a change in the location of the sound.

Since the above experiment did not directly involve speech, another experiment was performed dealing directly with speech

(Warren, Wagener & Herman, 1978). A tape recording was generated using four persons (2 male, 2 female) each reading excerpts from different prose passages. The recording was in stereo and created the sensation that the persons speaking were spatially arrayed in a row directly in front of the listener. Periodically a fifth male voice would be heard at a location directly in front of the listener. This voice would say "The word is (railroad or baseball or etc.)" in a slow, paced manner. Conventional spondee words such as "railroad" and "baseball" were used since they are easily heard. A subject was required to listen to the tape and report a best guess as to the spondee word that was spoken on that trial. The loudness level of the words spoken was adjusted up or down after every fifth trial in order to determine how loudly the words had to be spoken to be detected correctly. The tape recording had two sections, one was played in stereo and the other in monophonic to determine whether the subjects could use spatial information in the stereo condition to help screen out the interfering speech and focus on the location from which the speaker was saying the spondee word.

Older subjects did not benefit from the stereo condition. However, young adult subjects doubled their ability to hear the spondee words when the condition changed from monophonic to stereo.

Biofeedback

Increasing the alpha rhythm in the EEG has been associated with reduced levels of anxiety. Since older adults tend to produce less alpha activity than younger adults (Marsh & Thompson, 1977), a study was designed to assess whether increasing levels of alpha activity result in decreased levels of anxiety in older adults and whether the effect varies with age. A secondary issue was to investigate how effective biofeedback training would be in an adult population. The groups compared were (1) a biofeedback group; (2) a group receiving false biofeedback; and (3) a group receiving instructions on how to relax in addition to biofeedback.

Alpha activity was significantly increased only for the third group receiving biofeedback training in conjunction with simple relaxation training (Brannon, 1975). Moreover, anxiety levels and skin conductance levels were significantly reduced only in this group.

CONCLUSIONS

Information processing slows as persons grow older. However, all processes are not affected uniformly. Some stages of information processing seem to initiate specific ERP components. Thus, the timing of these ERP components can be used to measure some aspects of cognitive processes independent of other behavioral measures such as a keypress response. The experimental data indicate that many of the early stages of information processing are less affected by aging than the later stages associated with response selection and response execution.

Older adults are hampered more by having to obey complicated rules, or by making responses contrary to a long standing habit, than are young adults. However, this handicap may be overcome in part by a sufficient period of training to alter habits or to make complex situations more familiar.

The aging auditory system becomes less able to function efficiently because signal detection capability diminishes and an increasing level of self-generated "noise" occurs. Difficulty in decoding of speech is both a common and an important consequence of change in the human auditory system with age.

6

Social Factors in the Experience of Aging

When the First Longitudinal Study was planned, theory and methodology in social gerontology were not well developed. However, the dominant theoretical perspectives all stressed that social, contextual factors are important in understanding aging processes. This point had been made by E. W. Busse and his biomedical colleagues at the University of Colorado as they began to study age-related changes in brain functioning that were to stimulate the longitudinal studies at Duke.

A social history component became an integral part of plans for the Duke studies. Extensive data on social and demographic characteristics, interpersonal relationships, kinship, work, and perceived well-being were gathered. By the time the Second Longitudinal Study began in 1968, social gerontology had identified some key issues for which evidence from the Duke studies was particularly relevant. The intellectual context in which social scientific research in the Duke studies focused on person–environment interaction as fundamental for understanding human aging processes.

Disengagement theory was a prominent if not *the* prominent theoretical issue in social scientific research in the 1960s and well into the 1970s. During this same period what came to be called the age/period/cohort (APC) problem became a dominant methodological issue which also clearly had important theoretical implications for understanding the historical and social context of human aging.

Related to the APC issue was a new interest in age stratification and the allocation of societal resources by age. Finally, systematic social scientific and behavioral research in aging on stress emerged in the 1970s and intersected with renewed interest in age-related transitions and related life events. This intersection encouraged research on adaptation in later life to inevitable, age-related role transitions occasioned by retirement, changes in family structure, and illness.

This chapter will discuss briefly some of these major issues in the sociology of aging and, more generally, in social gerontology. Social scientific research on aging at Duke was more than responsive to these issues; the Duke Longitudinal Studies contributed to the clarification of (1) disengagement as an adaptive process in later life; (2) age stratification and its theoretical and methodological implications for understanding society as a succession of age-cohorts; and (3) the potentially stressful effects of normative role transitions and of social change in later life and the factors which predict successful adaptation to these changes. These theoretical issues identified the research problems to be investigated and influenced the design of the research pursued. For an extended discussion of these issues, see Palmore (1981).

CONCEPTUALIZATION AND DESIGN

The Problems

Disengagement

Disengagement theory attracted and deserved the attention it received in the 1960s. Grounding their theory in biology and in Erik Erikson's epigenetic principle of development, Cumming and Henry (1961) argued that an intrinsic and hence inevitable waning of physical and psychic energy initiates a process of individual withdrawal. This withdrawal, they argued, reinforced socially an individual's predisposition to withdraw because social groups recognize and communicate the necessity of redistributing roles and resources to their younger members. A mutual withdrawal of individuals and groups from one another, which might be perceived as mutual re-

jection, is more accurately perceived as both personally and socially desirable; hence, successful disengagement predicts not social
hostility or personal dissatisfaction but mutual satisfaction. Disengagement is, therefore, both universally a fact and is a personal and
social good.

Whether continued social engagement or reengagement was a
more accurate description of later life and more likely to produce
satisfactory personal and social outcomes was debated on its merits
for over a decade. An alternative proposal was that both the fact of
disengagement and the outcomes varied within and between societies; maintaining continuity of lifestyle, whether engaged or disengaged over the adult years, was more likely to be the fact and more
likely to produce a tolerable outcome (Havighurst, 1973; Maddox,
1964, 1965; Neugarten, 1964a&b; Atchley, 1972). Research in the
Duke studies addressed this problem directly. In so doing, the Duke
research addressed two related problems, the differentiation in social
characteristics which are observed in older adults of the same chronological age and the persistence of these differences over time.

Society as a Succession of Cohorts

The idea that society is usefully viewed as composed of age strata
that succeed one another over time is an old one in demographic
research. But the idea of age stratification of society received a formal expression and its implication for understanding the later years
within the life course were not elaborated until the 1970s (Riley,
Johnson & Foner, 1972). Age cohorts and age strata, e.g., may be
differently composed (cohorts may be large or small and with different educational experience), they may be exposed to social and
physical environments that are initially and subsequently different;
and they are likely to experience different societal allocations of roles
and resources. Differences in cohorts and in the composition of age
strata, in effect, are a reminder that aging is not only a biological process. Aging processes also involve historical and social factors. These
factors may and probably do ensure that successive cohorts of 60 year
olds are likely to be significantly different as they age and that un-
qualified assertions about universal aging processes based on cross-
sectional observations of particular samples of older adults are likely to be unjustified and misleading.

Age, Period, and Cohort

Understanding society as a succession of age cohorts within which biological, behavioral, social, and historical factors interact dynamically was at the heart of the age/period/cohort (APC) problem and attempts to disentangle the various components of aging processes in social scientific research. Conventional longitudinal research design, while it is a step in the right direction in research on aging, does not and cannot deal with APC issues satisfactorily. The experience of a particular cohort of older adults is not an adequate basis for broad generalizations about the universal experience of aging. Awareness of this underlay the cross-sequential design of the Second Longitudinal Study. Longitudinal design alone is not an altogether satisfactory response but it is a responsive step in the right direction.

Social Allocation of Resources

A dynamic view of age stratification has another important implication for research on aging. Different societies and any given society over time can and do develop different rules for allocating social roles and resources by age. Age prejudice and discrimination can and do occur and lead to the perception in our own society that older people constitute an unfavored minority group. Even if this is so, a dynamic view of age cohorts and the social complexity and diversity of their composition should make research investigators cautious. Social perceptions and allocation of resources over time can change. Hence, reference to *the elderly* and their universal experience are suspect *a priori* as are generalizations from the experiences of current cohorts of older adults to the probable experiences of future cohorts.

Role Transitions and Life Events

Role transitions and role loss are normatively expected experiences in later life. Change is expected in the later years and frequently occurs on schedule. The emergence and intersection in the 1970s of two theoretical perspectives—life events (e.g., Dohrenwend & Dohrenwend, 1974) and stress (e.g., House 1974)—were salutary for social scientific and behavioral research on aging. These perspectives were usefully incorporated in the analysis and interpretation of data from the Duke studies. Normative life events such as retirement, widowhood, changes in family structure, and serious illness are common events in later life which are potentially stressful but not necessarily so. The availability of physical, personal, and social resources constitute potentially important mediating variables. The dynamic multivariate perspective of stress theory, therefore, promised to increase understanding of whether and how various adaptive responses occur; this perspective was incorporated in the design of research in the second Duke study.

Research Design

The first study, in spite of its purposive sampling of volunteer subjects, was designed to include a broad spectrum of older persons living in a community context—males and females, Blacks and Whites, and persons with diverse socioeconomic backgrounds—so as to represent the distribution of these characteristics in the local population. The panelists could be located in social space with some precision; and with complementary evidence about psychological and biomedical characteristics ensured by a multidisciplinary research design, commonalities and diversities in the complex experience of growing older could be identified.

Longitudinal design also permitted the identification of continuities and changes in this experience for a defined panel of subjects. The multidisciplinary design facilitated the kinds of multivariate analysis that in recent decades have become standard in research on aging. Further, multidisciplinary design facilitated the documentation of the considerable diversity of older persons and of their experience of aging in terms of social integration, social involvement, family relationships, socioeconomic status, work, self-conception, and life satisfaction.

The second study was, as discussed in Chapter Two, designed to be cross-sequential and hence able to explore possible cohort differences in experience and the dynamics of responses to age-related life events. Together the first and second studies could address many of the basic methodological as well as theoretical issues that characterized social gerontological research over the past two decades.

FINDINGS

The findings highlighted here are presented in detail in Palmore (1981). The presentation is organized around major substantive issues and evidence from both the first and second studies is introduced as appropriate.

Social Integration and Involvement: Disengagement

Whether and how older adults maintain social integration and involvement and the personal effects of differential integration and involvement are the basic issues posed by disengagement theory. In regard to whether older persons tend to disengage as they grow older, evidence from both Duke studies is in agreement with the dominant conclusions from other research studies: levels of social interaction do tend to decrease with age for most older persons in many, but not all, types of activity (Maddox, 1965; Palmore, 1968). The proportion of retired persons clearly increases with age, and the amount of time in paid employment by those few who continue to work tends to decrease. Also total social activity tends, on average, to decline with age for both men and women. However, there is considerable variation in level and type of activity within and between age and sex groups at any one point in time; and variation in the amount and direction of change over time is observed.

There are also substantial minorities of older adults who maintain, redirect, or increase their social activity as they age. Furthermore, certain types of social activity do not seem to decline among participants in the Duke Studies. For example, no overall decline in club activities is apparent and there is a tendency to increase church attendance through the 60s, after which it levels off in the 70s and begins to decline only in later old age. Also, although the specific individuals in the social networks of older persons change, the total number of persons in these networks tends to remain constant. Thus, disengagement in the sense of substantial or total social isolation and inactivity was rare among the older adults studied in the Duke panels.

The majority of older persons did tend to decrease sexual activity, partly because of widowhood and partly because of declining health. But here too, there was a substantial minority who maintained or even increased their sexual activity (George & Weiler, 1981). Thus, while one basic hypothesis of disengagement theory (that older adults reduce activity and involvement) is generally true for most types of social activity, it is not true for substantial minorities of individuals and is not true of some types of activity.

The Duke studies do not provide a definitive test of Cumming and Henry's contention that the crucial change with age is the reduction of perceived life space and, presumably, the preference for this reduction. Behaviorally, the average older adult in the Duke panels maintained a relatively high level of activity. Whether disengagement or activity reduction contributes to better health, adjustment, and life satisfaction, can be addressed by the Duke studies more definitively.

Termination of employment (e.g., retirement) does not appear to have generally negative effects (Palmore, et al., 1979; George & Maddox, 1977). There appears to be no increase in physical or mental illness or in mortality caused by retirement. Nor does retirement generally tend to decrease life satisfaction; those few with a decrease in life satisfaction tend to be balanced by those with an increase. However, *involuntary* retirement does tend to have negative effects on life satisfaction, while return to work tends to have positive effects. In general, the fact of retirement appears to be less important than one's attitude toward work and what one does to compensate for loss of full-time employment.

The Duke studies found clear evidence that various forms of activity tend to contribute to and predict better health, happiness, and longevity (Palmore & Jeffers, 1971; Palmore & Luikart, 1972). The strongest social activity predictors of health and happiness were continuation of leisure activities, secondary group activities, interaction with people, and the total quantity of social activity. Greater longevity among men was predicted by work satisfaction and group activity, even after health and other factors were controlled.

Changes in family composition and relationships, often related to widowhood, tended to be associated with poorer health and less happiness among the middle-aged adults but not among the older panelists (Palmore, et al., 1979). Maintenance of sexual activity was associated with better health and happiness among both men and women, especially in the 50s and 60s, and is related to longevity (Palmore, 1981). Children leaving home did not typically produce long-term negative effects. In fact, the last child leaving home tended to increase reported life satisfaction and happiness for parents. On the other hand, children living nearby is associated with maintenance of life satisfaction among women as is having more friends nearby. Furthermore, number of friends was associated with better health among both men and women, although numbers of friends had no significant relationship to longevity (Palmore, 1981). Thus, the second basic hypothesis of disengagement theory is generally not true: Activity, not disengagement, tends to predict better life satisfaction, health, and longevity.

Among individuals who appear to be relatively disengaged, those who are least well integrated in a network of social relationships appear to have been relatively isolated over a number of years (Maddox, 1970). Further, over a series of longitudinal observations, when individuals are arrayed on a continuum of social involvement at a point in time, they tend to maintain their place in the rank order of social involvement over time (Maddox & Douglass, 1974). These data suggest an alternative to what has become a nonproductive stalemate in the argument about the factualness and consequences of disengagement and maintenance of social involvement. Individual older adults who are relatively disengaged or active are both observed over a broad range of ages. Maintenance of a preferred style in a social context which permits and facilitates that style is probably the critical issue. In the consideration of congruence between personal lifestyle and environmental opportunities, social context is also a variable; in a given society or social milieu there are differences in expectations about, in tolerance of, and in facilitation of disengagement and active involvement on the part of older persons.

Age Stratification

A number of findings from the Duke studies document and increase the understanding of age stratification and its implications for later life. Differences in the distribution of socio-economic status within and between age strata in the Duke panels reflected differences attributable to both age and cohort. The observed negative association between age and years of education completed, for example, is entirely due to cohort differences; the oldest cohorts in the longitudinal panels grew up in an era when lower educational attainment was the general experience. The lower occupational classification of older cohorts in the panels was also mainly a cohort effect, although some individuals may have drifted down to a lower status occupation in old age. The lower income of older cohorts is partly a cohort effect (i.e., as noted, due to their lower educational and occupational attainment) and partly an aging effect related to retirement and/or disability. However, the Duke Longitudinal Studies found less age-related decline in perceived adequacy of income than in amounts of income, and found no decline in perceived social status.

As for age stratification in employment, the percentage of older adults in the workforce in the United States has been decreasing among men but increasing among women in recent decades. This appears to be due primarily to period effects reflecting increasing availability of retirement benefits for men and the increasing labor force opportunities for women. The result has been that age stratification in employment has increased over time but the effect has been different for men and women.

The observed general decline in total social activity in the Duke panels reflects primarily aging effects. The increasing proportion of older cohorts married and living with spouse appears to reflect primarily increasing health and longevity of these cohorts rather than general period effects. This cohort effect on marital status and living arrangements is even stronger among men than women because longevity of women has been increasing more rapidly than that of men. Observed differences in longevity by sex ensures an increasingly high ratio of women to men in the future. Further, the number of single women will increase as the number of "never married" women and the number of divorced and separated women increase in younger cohorts of older persons. These changes reflect period effects.

There were few aging effects on life satisfaction or happiness observed among panelists followed longitudinally (Maddox, 1970). Those adults displaying decreases in satisfaction with age tended to be balanced by those displaying increases and, on average, in the array of panelists arranged on a continuum from high to low satisfaction, individuals tended to hold this place in rank. Therefore, some observed cross-sectional differences between age strata are primarily due to a mixture of the compositional effects within the age strata of samples studied and possibly of age, period, or cohort effects. Comparison of longitudinal and cross-sequential findings help sensitize investigators to why different conclusions are sometimes suggested by the two types of analysis.

Age, like occupation, gender, or ethnicity, is potentially a basis for societal allocation of valued roles and necessary resources. A great deal of social criticism and some research have stressed the probability that in modern societies the status and well-being of older persons will decline and that, in the United States as a case in point, older adults constitute a minority group subject to the prejudice and discrimination associated with such a status. From this perspective, old age becomes a "roleless role" and oldness evokes associated stereotypes of sickness, isolation, and poverty (Palmore, 1978b).

The Duke panels do not constitute samples from which provide definite refutation of negative stereotypes. But the Duke data do suggest why unrelievedly negative characterization should be viewed with caution and are probably more wrong than right, at least in the United States.

First, the characteristics of older adults in the Duke panels are quite varied and the observed variation in characteristics does not diminish with age (Maddox & Douglass, 1974). Second, the Duke panels present a relatively positive image of later life for both working class and middle class older adults. Admittedly, the Duke panels under-represent the lowest socioeconomic strata; but then again, these working class and middle class strata constitute a large proportion of older persons. The profile of the average older adult in the Duke studies of normal aging provides a positive image of health, social involvement, and satisfaction in later life. Cognitive functioning in the absence of illness remains relatively stable or declines moderately with age. And despite an overall decline in sexual activity with age, many older couples remain sexually interested and active at least into their 70s. Despite a high probability of potentially stressful events, longitudinal evidence documents capacity to adapt successfully to retirement, widowhood, children leaving home, and serious illness.

Third, although the Duke studies do not provide definitive evidence, the physical, behavioral, and social profile of the adult cohorts surviving to age 65 in the future can be expected to be better, not worse. The number of years of education completed continues to rise among adults; poverty among adults has tended to decline in recent decades. Smoking and consumption of high cholesterol diets and salt have declined among adults; adults are physically more active, and availability of medical care has increased.

A demonstrably favorable profile of older adults living in the community does not preclude negative stereotypes of aging embedded in cultural values. Stereotypes can and do persist in the face of contrary evidence. But the Duke studies suggest that reality testing on the part of older individuals and other adults tends to contradict widely shared negative imagery. Such imagery will appear increasingly arbitrary as the scientific evidence about aging in the United States is broadly disseminated. The days of an unambiguously negative image of older persons as a defenseless minority appear to be numbered.

Life Events and Stress

A longitudinal, cross-sequential analysis of response to several normative events in later life was carried out in the second study (Palmore et al., 1979). This analysis found, for example, that the event of retirement by itself does not usually produce unmanageable stress; successful adaptation is the usual outcome. Retirement did not appear to increase over-all morbidity or mortality, although sick people are more likely to retire than healthy people. Also, retirement did not appear to cause an increase in mental illness, certainly not among those who have moderate to high income and have been educated. Nor did retirement predict a decrease in life satisfaction; those who reported less satisfaction after retirement tended to be balanced by those who reported more satisfaction. However, *involuntary* retirement did tend to have negative effects on life satisfaction, adaptation, and activity. Return to work after retirement, on the other hand, tended to have positive effects.

When retirement is accompanied by sharp declines in perceived adequacy of income or by illness and disability, the result is more likely to produce decreased life satisfaction; but this decrease may be more the result of the declines in income and health than the result of retirement as such. A spouse's retirement appeared to have no significant negative effects.

The event of widowhood tended to be more stressful in late middle age than in old age as it produced lower satisfaction, lower income, more institutionalization, and higher morbidity and mortality rates; but the long-term effects, even in this group, were relatively small. Widowhood in old age appeared to have no measurable long-term negative effects. In fact, the death of a spouse in late life appeared to bring relief and improved adaptation for many who had been suffering through the ordeal of their spouse's disability and terminal illness.

Children leaving home did not usually produce long-term negative effects. In fact, the last child leaving home usually tended to increase rather than decrease happiness and life satisfaction among both men and women.

Major medical events (i.e., those requiring hospitalization) were associated with and produced the expected subsequent decline in health and some decline in activity. Such events, however, produced no significant long-term declines in any other measures of adaptation.

Thus, little evidence emerged from a longitudinal, cross-sequential analysis indicating that a single, specific life event was usually stressful enough to produce long-term negative effects in adaptation. However, there was evidence that the combination of several life events occurring close together is often stressful enough to produce negative outcomes. These effects appear to be additive so that the larger the number of events occurring, the larger the negative effects.

As for the effects of resources on adaptation to normative life events, psychological resources (such as intelligence and mental health) and social resources (such as higher socio-economic status and larger social networks) help to maintain health, happiness, and life satisfaction in the face of potentially stressful events. Greater personal health as a resource prior to illness appeared to help in returning to health after illness but did not appear to help in social-psychological adaptation.

Homogeneity and Heterogeneity

The observed variation in the experience of aging documented in the Duke studies warrants special emphasis. Some homogeneity was observed. Panelists, e.g., tended to become more homogeneous financially as their real incomes declined although considerable variation remained. Retirement probably appeared to have a two-stage effect on homogeneity of activities and life style. During the early 60's when some older persons are retiring but many are not, there is probably an increase in heterogeneity reflecting different expectations about and early experience in retirement (Stokes & Maddox, 1967). But in the later 60s when most have retired, increased homogeneity is observed, particularly in the report of successful adaptation. Differences between men and women panelists were observed since retirement clearly made the financial situation of men more like that of women, the majority of whom had not been working full-time in middle age.

In terms of social activities, previous research has reported conflicting results. The Duke studies found little evidence for either increasing homogeneity or heterogeneity, nor was there much evidence for greater or less similarity between men and women in social activities. Social networks of men as they retired became more similar to those of women and men became more dependent on family and friends for interaction. But widowhood tended to increase differences in social networks between men and women because women were more likely than men to experience the loss of a spouse.

Like retirement, sexual activity also appeared to involve two stages in later life. Heterogeneity tended to increase for adults in their 60s as some decreased their sexual activity and others did not; but for those in their 70s and 80s homogeneity increased as sexual activity, on average, declined significantly. Similarly, the differences between men and women in sexual activity tended to increase for those in their 60s as men expressed greater interest and reported more sexual activity than women. Then at older ages male/female differences declined as most of both sexes tended to become sexually inactive.

There was little evidence of any trend toward homogeneity or heterogeneity in life satisfaction, nor in differences between men and women in this characteristic. In general, life satisfaction remains, on average, relatively high in later life.

In a systematic analysis of variance in a broad range of physical, behavioral, and social indicators among panelists in the first study (Maddox & Douglass, 1974), maintenance of variability was documented. Further, on any array of characteristics, individuals tended to maintain their place in rank, suggesting the longitudinal continuity of characteristics.

CONCLUDING OBSERVATIONS

In summary, the Duke Longitudinal Studies have found considerable evidence which has helped to clarify and resolve some basic issues in gerontological research: on social integration; on age stratification; on the relationship among life events, stress; and on adaptation in later life. These findings were confirmed in research designed to include features of both longitudinal and cross-sequential design. Several important practical implications follow from the Duke studies.

The image of later life which emerged from the social scientific research suggested greater variability in the experience of aging and a more positive view of aging than prevailing stereotypes in the past three decades had suggested. Viewed longitudinally, panels of older adults living in the community demonstrated a capacity to adapt successfully to normative life course transitions. There is no reason to be pessimistic, but rather there is some basis for optimism that future cohorts of older persons will fare as well or better.

The potential for beneficial change in aging processes and in the experience of aging is of increasing interest. Research clearly is now in order on the factors which do or could reduce social prejudice and societal discrimination toward old adults. The more positive profiles expected for future cohorts of older adults should help and so should current legislation regarding job discrimination, access to health care, and income maintenance. Preparation for life transitions, particularly for retirement and widowhood, and the development of socially supportive environments could also be helpful.

The initial descriptive and experimental research of the Duke studies have anticipated an important current trend in research on aging, an interest in social intervention in aging processes and the experience of aging. The potential for change in later life and for beneficial changes in the experience of aging has been demonstrated.

7

In Retrospect and Prospect

Research projects have an ending as well as a beginning. In 1980 when the Duke longitudinal research team submitted a final report to the National Institute on Aging a quarter century after the studies began, there was a sense of relief as well as a sense of satisfaction. Scientific research is hard, frequently tedious, work. Multidisciplinary longitudinal research is particularly demanding. Maintaining the longitudinal records and the related multiple thousands of bits of information of interest to a variety of investigators in an adequately documented, retrievable form are as demanding as they are necessary and unglamorous. Insuring the continuity and motivation of a diverse multidisciplinary staff over many years is a challenge requiring considerable organizational and administrative ingenuity. The motivation and ethical treatment of longitudinal panelists on whom longitudinal research depends are tasks requiring continual attention.

In retrospect and on balance, the relief experienced at the termination of the Duke Longitudinal Studies was considerably outweighted by a sense of satisfaction. The sources of this satisfaction warrant comment. So do some of the implications of what was learned in research on aging at Duke for future research.

IMPORTANCE OF CONTEXT

Not all academic institutions and not all scientists are interested in multidisciplinary research on aging. Duke University leadership proved to be both interested and sympathetic at a time when interest

133

in aging as a societal and a scientific problem was uncommon. The university benefitted from the vision of a diverse group of scientists and scholars who anticipated the future correctly. This group included Philip Handler, a biochemist; E. W. Busse, a psychiatrist; Joseph Spengler, an economist and demographer; John McKinney, a sociologist; and Norman Garmenzy, a psychologist, among others. A University Council on Aging was created by the president of Duke to promote research and training throughout the university and to disseminate information about aging to broad professional, academic, and lay audiences. This council was instrumental in creating the Center for the Study of Aging and Human Development two years later and this Center provided the context in which the longitudinal studies developed and flourished.

The Duke Longitudinal Studies became the first sustained program of research in aging at the university and made the creation of a center possible. These studies also made the creation of a center necessary in order to achieve the critical mass of scientific investigators, laboratories, and financial resources necessary to sustain multidisciplinary longitudinal research.

The Center provided more than resources. It provided visibility and continuity in activities that helped ensure careers in aging for research investigators and clinicians and the exposure of research training fellows to the best theory and methodology available in the developing field of adult development and aging.

While the Duke Longitudinal Studies initially were the most visible program in the Duke Center, this did not remain so for very long. Over the years additional programs in basic and clinical research in aging emerged. Post-doctoral research training programs and geriatric training programs were developed. Clinical programs in geriatrics and programs focusing on applied, policy-oriented evaluative research were created.

The Center's Computing and Statistical Laboratory, its Social Survey Laboratory and related Data Archive, and its animal facility have proved to be especially important resources for research in aging not only for post-doctoral research fellows, visiting scholars, graduate students and honors undergraduates, but also for experienced investigators at Duke and at other institutions in the United States and abroad. Placing the data tapes and documentation of the longitudinal studies in the public domain through the Center's Data Archive, for example, has insured the availability of these data for future generations of scientific investigators and expanded enormously the network of investigators with whom research investigators at Duke interact.

CAREER DEVELOPMENT IN AGING

Sustained, visible commitment of Duke University to gerontology and geriatrics has had a beneficial effect on career development of scientists at Duke committed to research, training, and the application of research on service. Most of the members of the initial longitudinal research team were or became tenured members of the faculty. Participation in the longitudinal studies was, and was perceived to be, an important vehicle for career development in aging.

Career development in aging was clearly enhanced by sound administrative management of the Duke studies. Investigators met weekly to plan and review implementation of the longitudinal studies and were involved in making decisions designed to make the studies productive. They learned how to do multidisciplinary longitudinal research by being actively involved in it. Investigators were given responsibility for and control of data in the domain of their expertise. They were encouraged to and assisted in the regular publication of findings in journals of their disciplines rather than delaying publication until the project was completed. This career development strategy exacted a price; publications were scattered in a wide range of journals, a fact that prompted this volume as an attempt to provide the highlights of the studies and a guide to where detailed information can be located. But the effect on career development was, overall, beneficial for a large number of research investigators, clinicians, and teachers as the large number of colleagues listed in the acknowledgements of this volume indicates.

ON THEORY IN AGING

The Duke Longitudinal Studies began without benefit of a master theory of human aging. They ended without producing one and without compelling reasons for believing that a single, sovereign theory of aging would currently be possible or useful. Organizing a comprehensive research study around a master theory of aging was not an option a quarter century ago; no very promising candidate was available to provide the single intellectual peg on which to hang the research of biomedical, behavioral and social scientists studying aging processes and the experience of aging.

To the scientists who planned and implemented the initial longitudinal study at Duke, the urgently and practically useful immediate tasks were to develop normative descriptions of the various dimensions of aging processes, to document the interrelation of biomedical, behavioral and social variables, to generate hypotheses, and, insofar as possible, to test hypotheses suggested by various partial theories of different disciplines. In the interest of assembling and maintaining a team of investigators willing to work on a common enterprise, over presumably a long period of time, forcing them to rally around a single theoretical perspective did not seem wise at the outset. In retrospect, this pragmatic decision still seems to have been the right one.

Although the longitudinal research team did not share a single common theory, they did share a common theoretical perspective. This perspective, which became more explicit over time, conceived aging processes and the experience of aging as products of a dynamic interaction between individuals—both as biological organisms and as social beings—and social contexts. Within some broad and unspecified limits, aging processes and the experience of aging are demonstrably not fixed and immutable. These processes and experiences are dynamically interconnected and they are modifiable. What justifies such a conclusion?

Societies are usefully conceived as large-scale natural experiments in which aging processes and the experience of aging potentially have very different outcomes. Historically and currently, average life expectancy and age- and gender-specific mortality rates are both strikingly different and changing. The diseases which impair, disable and handicap Americans today are not the same as they were fifty years ago. Illness and death among older people in developing counties is still caused primarily from conditions related to malnutrition, poor hygiene, and pest-borne disease that are socially modifiable. Health impairment among adults in the United States currently is substantially attributable to risk factors—conditions such as nutritional habits, use of cigarettes and drugs, lack of exercise, and stress which predict unwanted outcomes—that are primarily attributable to learned, socially reinforced behavior and lifestyles rather than to biology, access to health care, or hostile physical environment.

If one broadens the concept of health to include personal and social well-being, one finds it easy to broaden the risk factors that change the probability of survival and the maintenance of personal and social well-being in the later years to include poverty, ignorance, and social deprivation. Society-as-experiment is particularly well illustrated by the way in which any given society stratifies itself and allocates roles and resources by age, gender, and social status. There is no natural law or scientific theory that requires the organization of social institutions to ensure that older persons are over-represented among those who are impoverished, poorly educated, retired early, or subjected to prejudice and discrimination. Placement at the bottom of a social stratification system of a society, historically and presently, is a powerful predictor of survival and well-being among adults. That this is so and why it is so can be demonstrated. Why this continues to be the case requires an understanding of societal values and political processes.

Once this is understood, tasks of scientific research and theory in aging become clearer. The essential task of research is to specify and explain the effects on aging processes and the experience of aging resulting from the large variety of natural contexts in which aging is observed to occur. These are the effects that produce secondary aging processes which are superimposed upon and which modify primary biological processes. Differentiating primary and secondary processes of human aging was the task on which the longitudinal studies at Duke began to work. A related task was to identify and explain the stability and change in the biological, behavioral, and social potential of adults over time, isolating insofar as possible primary aging processes as they might be observed under theoretically optimal conditions.

The Duke Longitudinal Studies provides a description of normative aging processes and the experience of aging observed in two panels of older adults living in the community. Variations in the biological, behavioral, and social aspects of aging were clearly documented among persons of the same chronological age. Knowing that an adult is 65, 70, or 75 years of age proved to be a relatively weak predictor of functional health status, of cognitive performance, of social integration, or of successful adaptation to role transitions. Predicting the observed outcomes of aging were more adequately and accurately done by conceptualizing aging as a multivariate process in which the connectedness and dynamic interaction of its dimensions are included. Health status does affect cognitive performance; but so does education, and education is related to the social location of an individual in different cohorts over the life course.

In the Duke studies, potentially stressful events related to life transitions were not equally distributed among older adults. And more importantly, successful adaptation to life events was mediated by the availability of social as well as biological and personal resources. The Duke studies demonstrated the necessity of studying modifiable human aging in a variety of contexts and the benefits of doing so.

The implication for theory of a multidimensional, contextual approach to aging is that one can begin specifying the conditions under which maximal longevity, functional capacity, adaptive capacity, and sense of well-being occur or might occur. Societies as natural experiments have provided some insights into the different conditions which produce different outcomes. Research at Duke on the outcomes of different socially learned and reinforced behavior and lifestyle on aging processes has been useful. Biological and biomedical research has produced useful information on how the human body might be assisted in operating more efficiently for a longer period of time.

More adequate theory specifying the conditions of optimal biological aging, psychological aging and social aging is clearly in prospect. But a comprehensive theory of optimal aging is less clearly in prospect for several reasons.

One can imagine, for example, a theory of optimal biological survival and a theory of optimal behavior, personality, cognition and lifestyle that complements biological theory. Further, one can imagine—but with more difficulty—a complementary theory of optimum social aging specifying the timing of life course transitions, the behavior and lifestyles to be taught and reinforced, and the allocation of societal resources by age.

A comprehensive theory of aging specifying the interconnectedness of these dimensions of aging processes and experience would be useful as a model for assessing aging as it is observed normatively and as it might be observed optimally. If such a theoretically derived model were achieved, at least two outcomes would be predictable. The first, societal values and related preferences will ensure different assessments of the social capability and desirability of meeting the conditions of optimal aging. This implies that a theory of optimum aging would require and benefit from a socio-political theory of how individuals and groups perceive and respond to scientific information affecting their values, behavior, and lifestyles in fundamental ways. The second predicted outcome is that observed attempts to approximate a model of optimal aging would always be approximate, and hence sub-optimal; a variety of possible solutions will be found to work equally well. A variety of tradeoffs, particularly societal negotiations about the distribution of resources over the life course, would have to be made by individuals and social groups to achieve simultaneously maximum life expectancy and reasonable assurance of personal and societal well-being. Individuals and social groups, for example, would have to be willing to modify and control behavior and lifestyles. The scientific capacity for constructing or reconstructing the life course transitions and the allocation of societal resources in ways that might improve longevity and well-being are no longer hypothetical possibilities; they are real. The desirability of constructing the future of aging and the political capacity to do so remain debatable.

A comprehensive theory of human aging scientific theory that describes, explains, and predicts is also available for experimentation and controls. However, a comprehensive theory of aging, if it existed, would go far beyond science and the social function it is currently perceived to have. A comprehensive theory of aging would have to specify optimal social environments. The construction of such environments is primarily a political, not a scientific, task.

THE FUTURE OF RESEARCH IN AGING

The implications of continual interaction among aging, periods of measurement (as an index of environment) and cohorts (collectivities which are the repositories of past experience of individuals which affect future responses to environments) are revolutionary. Disciplinary studies of aging processes and of the experience of aging in experimental and naturalistic contexts will continue to contribute to scientific understanding of specific aspects of aging. Normative studies of aging in defined populations will also continue to make a contribution in specifying observed continuities and changes. But, in the future, the limitations of time-bound, culture-bound, and population-specific research for identifying and explicating universal processes of primary aging and the principles for understanding universals in the experience of aging will certainly become increasingly obvious.

General purpose, multidisciplinary longitudinal studies of aging of the kind exemplified by the Duke Longitudinal Studies are unlikely to be undertaken again. We have learned a great deal about aging and the experience of aging from such studies. But we have also learned the limitations of what can be learned and have learned the high cost of such research.

Some potentially useful guidelines for future research on aging emerge from the Duke Longitudinal Studies. First, a great deal of information relevant for understanding aging processes now exists and this information is under-utilized. While the research team responsible for the Duke Longitudinal Studies have a relatively good record of exploiting the data collected over a period of two decades, a great deal remains to be done and much more than can conceivably be done by the initial investigators. This is one of the compelling reasons for placing the data sets of the Duke studies in the public domain in accessible form for use by colleagues at Duke and at other institutions. The accessibility of the data sets also increases the potential of their use by graduate students, post-doctoral research fellows, and visiting scholars.

Second, adequate research on aging in the future will necessarily emphasize comparative study of different age cohorts in the same society and of aging populations in different societies. In the immediate future, large-scale comparative research on aging in different societies will be prohibited by cost alone. But, in the interim some useful comparative cross-national research is already being illustrated in demography and epidemiology, which benefit from a relatively standardized set of measurement procedures and data sources.

Comparative research within societies is also increasingly possible as investigators identify data relevant for investigating aging processes gathered with the same, similar or complementary measurement procedures. The Wechsler Adult Intelligence Scale (WAIS), for example, has been widely used in research on cognitive functioning of aging in a variety of studies. The evidence from these studies is now being collated and compared. Similarly, a number of studies have used relatively standardized procedures for assessing cardiovascular functioning in later life, studies as apparently unrelated in initial objectives as the Duke Longitudinal Studies, the Framingham Studies of Heart Disease, and the Evans County Study of Heart Disease. The potential complementarity of these studies for an understanding of cardiovascular functioning in later life is now being explored. International studies of self-care capacity (Activities of Daily Living) are now possible. These are but three illustrations of new interests in exploring the complementarity of existing data sets for understanding aging processes.

Third, adequate research on aging in the future will continue to benefit from multidisciplinary interaction. This does not mean that important research in aging will not be done by scientists with distinctly disciplinary orientations working only narrowly defined problems of basis research. Quite the contrary. Experience with the Duke Longitudinal Studies illustrates the contribution of specifically focused ancillary studies to supplement the major commitment to multidisciplinary study of defined panels of older adults. Important disciplinary issues in basic research cannot always be anticipated by and dictated by the demands of a multidisciplinary research team with their own distinctive interests, however legitimate those interests are.

The intellectual autonomy of disciplines on research on aging exacts its own price. If processes of aging and the experience of aging are determined by multiple factors as persons and environments interact, as is certainly the case, it is difficult to imagine that biologists and biomedical scientists would not profit eventually from interaction with behavioral and social scientists—and vice versa. Ultimately, normative processes of aging, in the sense of universal processes, will never be established independently of assessing the aging of individuals in the context of the environments in which they live.

Laboratory experiments can tell, at best, only part of the story.

Finally, research on aging in the future will be directed increasingly to testing the limits of modifying currently observed processes of aging and the experience of aging. "If you want to understand something, try to change it" is an old maxim of experimental and clinical science. The idea that aging processes are immutable can no longer be defended. Key questions for aging research in the future will, therefore, concentrate on the limits of modifiability of aging processes and the implications, both personal and societal, of the changes that scientists can imagine and, if given the opportunity, might produce. The ethical issues involved in modifying processes of aging and the experience of aging are complex and whether social consensus exists or might emerge regarding changes that are perceived to be both possible and desirable remains to be demonstrated.

We should not delay in our discussion of this issue. Societies are already experimenting, though not always deliberately and consciously, in ways that are changing the age composition of populations and the allocation of resources across the life course. Biomedical science is suggesting and implementing ways to modify patterns of morbidity and longevity.

The future of aging is currently being reconstructed. Scientific research can help define the limits of the possible and provide the tools. Science, however, cannot define the future of aging to which individuals and societies ought to aspire.

References

Anderson, B., and Palmore, E. Longitudinal evaluation of ocular function. In E. Palmore (Ed.), *Normal Aging II*. Durham, N.C.: Duke University Press, 1974, 24–32.

Atchley, R. *Social Forces in Later Life*. Belmont, Ca.: Wadsworth, 1972.

Back, K. W. Transition to aging and the self-image. *Aging and Human Development*, 1971, 2, 296–304. Reprinted in E. Palmore (Ed.), *Normal Aging II*. Durham, N.C.: Duke University Press, 1974, 207–216.

Back, K. W., and Bourque, L. Life graphs: Aging and cohort effect. *Journal of Gerontology*, 1970, 35, 249–255.

Back, K. W., and Gergen, K. J. The self through the latter span of life. In C. Gordon and K. J. Gordon (Eds.), *The Self in Social Interaction*. New York: Wiley, 1968.

Back, K. W., and Morris, J. D. Perception of self and the study of whole lives. In E. Palmore (Ed.), *Normal Aging II*. Durham, N.C.: Duke University Press, 1974, 216–221.

Back, K. W., and Sullivan, D. A. Self-image, medicine, and drug use. *Addictive Diseases: An International Journal*, 1978, 3, 373–382.

Baddeley, A. D. *The Psychology of Memory*. Basic Books, New York, 1976.

Barnes, R. H., Busse, E. W., and Friedman, E. L. Psychological functioning of aged individuals with normal and abnormal electroencephalograms: A study of hospitalized individuals. *Journal of Nervous Mental Diseases*, 1956, 124, 585–593.

Beck, E. C., Dustman, R. E., and Schenkenberg, T. Life span changes in the electrical activity of the human brain as reflected in the cerebral evoked response. In J. M. Ordy and K. R. Brizzee (Eds.), *Neurobiology of Aging*. New York: Plenum, 1975, 175–192.

Botwinick, J. Cautiousness in advanced age. *Journal of Gerontology*, 1966, *21*, 347–353.

Botwinick, J. Intellectual abilities. In J. E. Birren and K. W. Schaie (Eds.), *Handbook of the Psychology of Aging*. New York: Van Nostrand Reinhold Co., 1977, 580–605.

Botwinick, J., and Siegler, I. C. Intellectual ability among the elderly: Simultaneous cross-sectional and longitudinal comparisons. *Developmental Psychology*, 1980, *16*:1, 49–53.

Bourque, L., and Back, K. W. The middle years as seen through the life graph. *Sociological Symposium*, 1969, *1*, 19–29.

Bourque, L., and Back, K. W. Life graphs and life events. *Journal of Gerontology*, 1977, *32*, 669–674.

Brannon, L. J. The effect of increased alpha production on the psychological function of the elderly. Unpublished doctoral dissertation, Pennyslvania State University, 1975.

Brehm, M. L., and Back, K. W. Self-image and attitudes toward drugs. *Journal of Personality*, 1968, *36*, 229–314.

Breytspraak, L. M. The impact of achievement on the self-concept of middle-older-aged adults. Doctoral dissertation. Durham, N.C.: Duke University, 1973.

Buckley, C. E., and Dorsey, F. C. Serum immunoglobulin concentrations in an older population. *Journal of Immunology*, 1970, *4*, 964–972.

Busse, E. W. The treatment of the chronic complainer. *Medical Record Annals*, 1956, *1*, 196–200.

Busse, E. W. Hypochondriasis in the elderly: A reaction to social stress. *Journal of American Geriatric Society*, 1976, *24*, 145–149.

Busse, E. W. Duke Longitudinal Study I: Senescence and senility. In R. Katzman, R. D. Terry, and K. L. Bick (Eds.), *Alzheimer's Disease: Senile Dementia and Related Disorders* (*Aging*, Vol. 7). New York: Raven Press, 1978, 59–68.

Busse, E. W., Dovenmuehle, R. H., and Brown, R. G. Psychoneurotic reactions of the aged. *Geriatrics*, 1960, *14*, 97–105.

Busse, E. W., and Obrist, W. D. Presenscent electroencephalographic changes in normal subjects. *Journal of Gerontology*, 1965, *20*, 315–320.

Busse, E. W., and Wang, H. S. Multiple factors contributing to dementia in old age. In E. Palmore (Ed.), *Normal Aging II*. Durham, N.C.: Duke University Press, 1974a, 151–160.

Busse, E. W., and Wang, H. S. Heart disease and brain impairment among aged persons. In E. Palmore (Ed.), *Normal Aging II*. Durham, N.C.: Duke University Press, 1974b, 160–167.

Busse, E. W., and Wang, H. S. The electroencephalographic changes in late life: A longitudinal study. *Journal of Clinical and Experimental Gerontology*, 1979, *1*, 145–158.

Busse, E. W., Barnes, R. H., Silverman, A. J., Thaler, M., and Frost, L. R. Studies of the processes of aging: Factors that influence the psyche of elderly persons. *American Journal of Psychiatry*, 1954, *110*, 897–903.

Cameron, P. Masculinity—femininity in the aged. *Journal of Gerontology*, 1968, *10*, 63–65.

Cattell, R. B. *Handbook Supplement for Form C of the 16 Personality Factor Test.* 2nd Edition. Champaign, Ill.: Institute for Personality and Ability Testing, 1962.

Cattell, R. B., Eber, H. W., and Latsuka, M. M. *Handbook for the 16 Personality Factor Questionnaire (16PF)*. Champaign, Ill.: Institute for Personality and Ability Testing, 1970.

Cleveland, W. P., Hamilton, R. D., and Ramm, D. A User's Guide to Missing Data Estimation, Technical Report of the Duke Center Survey Data Laboratory and Archive, 1978.

Clive, J. M. Use of the DITTO and GOM Computational Algorithms Technical Memorandum, Department of Biomathematics, Duke University Medical Center, August 1, 1978.

Clive, J., Woodbury, M., and Siegler, I. Fuzzy and crisp set-theoretic-based classification of health and disease. *Journal of Medical Systems*, 7:317–332, 1983.

Corbett, J. L., and Eidelman, B. H. An evaluation of the xenon inhalation technique for the measurement of cerebral blood flow. Paper presented at the Sixth International Symposium on Cerebral Blood Flow and Metabolism, Philadelphia, 1973.

Craik, F. I. M. Age differences in human memory. In J. E. Birren and K. W. Schaie (Eds.), *Handbook of the Psychology of Aging*. New York: Van Nostrand Reinhold Co., 1977, 384–420.

Cronback, L., and Furby, L. How should we measure change, or should we? *Psychological Bulletin*, 1970, *74*, 68–80.

Cumming, E., and Henry, W. *Growing Old: The Process of Disengagement*. New York: Basic Books, 1961.

Dempster, A. P., Laird, N. M., and Rubin, D. B. Maximum Likelihood From Incomplete Data Via the EM Algorithm (with discussion), *JRSS* B *39*, 1977, 1–38.

Dohrenwend, B. J., and Dohrenwend, B. P. (Eds.). *Stressful Life Events*. New York: John Wiley, 1974.

Doppelt, J. E., and Wallace, W. L. Standardization of the Wechsler Adult

Intelligence Scale for older persons. *Journal of Abnormal and Social Psychology*, 1955, *51*, 312–330.

Dowdy, L. W. A Problem and Program Involving Missing Data Analysis, Department of Computer Science, Duke University CS-1975-13.

Duke Computation Center, TSAR User's Manual, 1974.

Eisdorfer, C. Developmental level sensory impairment in the aged. *Journal of Projective Techniques and Personality Assessment*, 1960a, *24*, 129–132.

Eisdorfer, C. Rorschach rigidity and sensory decrement in a senescent population. *Journal of Gerontology*, 1960b, *15*, 188–190.

Eisdorfer, C. The WAIS performance of the aged: A retest evaluation. *Journal of Gerontology*, 1963, *18*, 169–172.

Eisdorfer, C., and Cohen, D. The generality of the WAIS standardization for the aged. *Journal of Abnormal and Social Psychology*, 1961, *62*, 520–527.

Eisdorfer, C., and Wilkie, F. Auditory change. In E. Palmore (Ed.), *Normal Aging II*. Durham, N.C.: Duke University Press, 1974a, 32–41.

Eisdorfer, C., and Wilkie, F. Intellectual changes. In E. Palmore (Ed.), *Normal Aging II*. Durham, N.C.: Duke University Press, 1974b, 95–103.

Elias, M. F., and Kinsbourne, M. Age and sex differences in the processing of verbal and nonverbal stimuli. *Journal of Gerontology*, 1974, *29*, 162–171.

Fox, J. H. Women, Work, and Retirement. Doctoral dissertation. Durham, N. C.: Duke University, 1975.

Fox, J. H. Effects of retirement and former work life on women's adaptation in old age. *Journal of Gerontology*, 1977, *32*, 196–202.

Gaylord, S. A., and Marsh, G. R. Age differences in the speed of a spatial cognitive process. *Journal of Gerontology*, 1975, *30*, 674–678.

George, L. K. Subjective Awareness of Self and Age in Middle and Late Life. Doctoral dissertation. Durham, N.C.: Duke University, 1975.

George, L. K., and Maddox, G. L. Subjective adaptation to loss of the work role: A longitudinal study. *Journal of Gerontology*, 1977, *32*(4), 456–462.

George, L. K. The impact of personality and social status factors upon levels of activity and psychological well-being. *Journal of Gerontology*, 1978, *33*, 840–847.

George, L. K., and Siegler, I. C. Coping with stress and challenge in later life. Grant proposal submitted to NRTA–AARP. Andrus Foundation, 1979.

George, L. K., Siegler, I. C., and Okun, M. A. Separating age, cohort, and time of measurement: Analysis of variance or multiple regression. *Experimental Aging Research*, 1981, *7*:3, 299–314.

George, L. K., and Weiler, S. J. Sexuality in middle and late life: The effects of age, cohort, and gender. *Archives of General Psychiatry*, 1981, *38*, 919–923.

Gianturco, D. L., and Busse, E. W. Psychiatric problems encountered during a long-term study of normal aging volunteers. In A. D. Isaacs and F. Post (Eds.), *Studies in Geriatric Medicine*. Chichester, UK: John Wiley and Sons, Ltd., 1978, 1–16.

Gibbs, F. A., and Gibbs, E. L. *Atlas of Electroencephalography: Methodology and Controls*. Cambridge: Addison-Wesley Press, 1950.

Guttman, D. The cross-cultural perspective: Notes toward a comparative psychology of aging. In J. E. Birren and K. W. Schaie (Eds.), *Handbook of the Psychology of Aging*. New York: Van Nostrand Reinhold Co., 1977, 302–326.

Hall, J. W., III. Elements of timbre perception. *T.-I.-T. Journal of Life Sciences*, 1977, *7*, 43–51.

Hall, J. W., III. The effects of subject age and complexity of stimulus on evoked brainstem responses. Paper presented at the 95th annual meeting of the Acoustical Society of America, 1978.

Hall, J. W., III. Auditory brainstem frequency following responses to waveform envelope periodicity. *Science*, 1979, *205*, 1297–1299.

Hall, J. W., III, and Soderquist, D. R. Adaptation of residual pitch. *Journal of the Acoustical Society of America*, 1978, *63*, 883–893.

Harkins, S. W., Nowlin, J. B., Ramm, D., and Schroeder, S. Effects of age, sex, and time-on-watch on a brief continuous performance task. In E. Palmore (Ed.), *Normal Aging II*. Durham, N.C.: Duke University Press, 1974, 140–150.

Havighurst, R. Social roles, work, leisure, and education. In C. Eisdorfer and M. Lawton (Eds.), *The Psychology of Adult Development and Aging*. Washington: APA, 1973.

Herman, G. E., Warren, L. R., and Wagener, J. W. Auditory lateralization: Age differences in sensitivity to dichotic time and amplitude cues. *Journal of Gerontology*, 1977, *32*, 187–191.

Hock, H. S., and Egeth, H. E. Verbal interference with encoding in a perceptual classification task. *Journal of Experimental Psychology*, 1970, *83*, 299–303.

Horn, T. L. Organization of abilities and the development of intelligence. *Psychological Review*, 1968, *75*, 242–259.

Horn, T. L. Organization of data on life span development of human abilities. In L. R. Goulet and P. B. Bates (Eds.), *Life Span Developmental Psychology: Research and Theory*. New York: Academic Press, 1970, 423–466.

House, J. Occupation stress and coronary heart disease. *Journal of Health and Social Behavior*, 1974, *15*, 12–27.

Jasper, H. H. The ten-twenty system of the International Federation of Societies for EEG and clinical neurophysiology. *Electroencephalography and Clinical Neurophysiology*, 1958, *10*:2, 371–378.

Kleemeier, R. W. Intellectual changes in the senium or death and IQ. Paper presented at the annual meeting of the American Psychological Association, New York, September, 1961.

Kleemeier, R. W. Intellectual changes in the senium. *Proceedings of the American Statistical Association*, 1962, *1*, 290–295.

Kooi, K. W., Guverner, G. M., Lupper, C. J., and Bagchi, B. K. Electroencephalographic patterns of the temporal region in normal adults. *Neurology*, 1964, *14*, 1029–1035.

Kutas, M., McCarthy, G., and Donchin, E. Augmenting mental chronometry: The P_{300} as a measure of stimulus evaluation time. *Science*, 1977, *197*, 792–795.

Lowenthal, M. F. Social and related factors leading to psychiatric hospitalization of the aged. *American Geriatrics Society*, 1965, *13*, 110–112.

Madden, D. J., and Nebes, R. D. Aging and the development of automaticity in visual search. *Developmental Psychology*, 1980a, *16*, 377–384.

Madden, D. J., and Nebes, R. D. Visual perception and memory. In M. C. Wittrock (Ed.), *The Brain and Psychology*. New York: Academic Press, 1980b.

Maddox, G. L. Disengagement theory: A critical evaluation. *Gerontologist*, 1964, *4*, 80–83.

Maddox, G. L. Fact and Artifact. *Human Development*, 1965, *8*, 117–180.

Maddox, G. L. Persistence in lifestyle of the elderly. In E. Palmore (Ed.), *Normal Aging*. Durham, N.C.: Duke University Press, 1970a.

Maddox, G. L. A longitudinal, multidisciplinary study of human aging. *Proceedings of the American Statistical Association*, 1962, 280–285. Reprinted in E. B. Palmore (Ed.), *Normal Aging*. Durham, N.C.: Duke University Press, 1970b, 18–27.

Maddox, G. L., and Campbell, R. Scope, concepts, and methods in the study of aging. In R. Binstock and E. Shanas (Eds.), *Handbook of Aging and the Social Sciences*. (Second Edition). New York: Van Nostrand Reinhold, 1985.

Maddox, G. L., and Douglass, E. Aging and individual differences. *Journal of Gerontology*, 1974, *29*(3), 555–563.

Maddox, G. L., and Wiley, J. Scope, concepts, and methods in the study of aging. In R. Binstock and E. Shanas (Eds.), *Handbook of Aging and the Social Sciences*. New York: Van Nostrand Reinhold, 1976.

Madow, W. G. (Ed.) *Incomplete Data in Survey Samples*. Vol. 3, Session IV. Academic Press, 1983.

Marsh, G. R. Age differences in evoked potential correlates of a memory scanning process. *Experimental Aging Research*, 1975, *1*, 3–16.

Marsh, G. R. Changes in cognitive performance and evoked potential correlates to pharmacologic intervention in the elderly. In L. W. Poon and J. L. Fozard (Eds.), *Design Conference on Decision Making and Aging*. Technical Report 76-01, Normative Aging Study and Bedford/Boston Geriatric Research Educational and Clinical Center, 1976a, 238–256.

Marsh, G. R. Electrophysiological correlates of aging and behavior. In M. F. Elias, B. E. Eleftheriou, and P. K. Elias (Eds.), *Special Review of Experimental Aging Research: Progress in Biology*. Bar Harbor, Maine: EAR, Inc., 1976b, 165–178.

Marsh, G. R. Aging effects on the human evoked potential. In D. A. Otto (Ed.), *Multidisciplinary Perspectives in Event-Related Brain Potential Research*. Washington, D.C.: U.S. Government Printing Office, 1978, 333–336.

Marsh, G. R., and Linnoila, M. The effects of deanol on cognitive performance and electrophysiology in elderly humans. *Psychopharmacology*, 1979, *66*, 99–104.

Marsh, G. R., and Thompson, L. W. The psychophysiology of aging. In J. E. Birren and K. W. Schaie (Eds.), *Handbook of the Psychology of Aging*. New York: Van Nostrand Reinhold Co., 1977, 219–248.

Marsh, G. R., and Watson, W. E. Psychophysiological studies of aging effects on cognitive processes. In D. G. Stein (Ed.), *The Psychobiology of Aging: Problems and Perspectives*. New York: Elsevier/North Holland, 1980, 395–410.

Marsh, G. R., Poon, L. W., and Thompson, L. W. Some relationships between CNV, P_{300} and task demands. In W. C. McCallum and J. R. Knott (Eds.), *The Responsive Brain*. Briston, U.K.: John Wright & Sons, Ltd., 1976, 122–125.

Mason, K., and Mason, W. Some methodological issues in cohort analysis of archival data. *American Sociological Review*, 1973, *38*, 242–258.

McAdam, W., Tait, A. C., and Orme, J. E. Initial psychiatric illness in involuntary women—III. *Journal of Mental Science*, 1957, *103*, 824–829.

McCarty, S. M., Siegler, I. C., and Logue, P. E. Cross-sectional and longitudinal patterns of three Wechsler memory scale subtests. *Journal of Gerontology*, 1982, *37*(2), 169–175.

Milner, B. Hemispheric specialization: Scope and Limits. In F. G. Worden and F. O. Schmitt (Eds.), *The Neurosciences: Third Study Program*. Cambridge: MIT Press, 1974, 75–89.

Molfese, D. L. (Ed.). Neuroelectrical correlates of language processes: Evidence from scalp recorded evoked potential research. *Brain and Language*, 1980, *11*, 235–307.

Moscovitch, M. Information processing and the cerebral hemispheres. In M. S. Gazzaniga (Ed.), *Handbook of Behavioral Neurobiology* (Vol. 2). New York: Plenum Press, 1979.

Muller, H. F., Grad, B., and Engelsmann, F. Biological and psychological predictors of survival in a psychogeriatric population. *Journal of Gerontology*, 1975, *30*, 47–52.

Mundy-Castle, A. C. Central excitability in the aged. In H. T. Blumenthal (Ed.), *Medical and Clinical Aspects of Aging*. New York: Columbia University Press, 1962, 575–595.

Nebes, R. D. Verbal-pictorial recording in the elderly. *Journal of Gerontology*, 1976, *31*, 421–427.

Nebes, R. D. Vocal versus manual response as a determinant of age difference in simple reaction time. *Journal of Gerontology*, 1978, *33*, 884–889.

Nebes, R. D., and Andrews-Kulis, M. F. The effect of age on the speed of sentence formation and incidental learning. *Experimental Aging Research*, 1976, *2*, 315–331.

Nebes, R. D., and Elias, C. The effect of verbal labelling on the recognition of random shapes by elderly and young adults. Unpublished data, Duke Center for the Study of Aging, 1978.

Nebes, R. D., Madden, D. J., and Berg, W. D. The effect of age on hemispheric asymmetry in visual and auditory identification. Manuscript submitted for publication, 1981.

Neugarten, B. *Personality in Middle and Late Life*. New York: Atherton Press, 1964a.

Neugarten, B. A developmental view of adult personality. In J. Birren (Ed.), *Relations of Development and Aging*. Springfield, Ill.: Thomas, 1964b.

Nie, N., Hull, C. H., Jenkins, J. G., Steinbrenner, K., and Bent, D. H. *SPSS, Statistical Package for the Social Sciences*, 2nd edition, McGraw Hill, 1975.

Nowlin, J. B. Anxiety during a medical examination. In E. Palmore (Ed.), *Normal Aging II*. Durham, N.C.: Duke University Press, 1974, 78–86.

Nowlin, J. B. Cigarette use and cardiovascular disease in middle and late life. *Proceedings of the 11th International Congress of Gerontology*, Tokyo, Japan, 1978, 90 (abstract).

Nowlin, J. B. Vibratory threshold in a middle-aged and elderly population.

Journal of Gerontology, 1980, in press.

Nowlin, J. B., Eisdorfer, C., and Bates, E. A longitudinal appraisal of serum cholesterol in a geriatric population. *Proceedings of the 8th International Congress of Gerontology,* Washington, D. C., 1969, Vol. 2, 46 (abstract).

Nowlin, J. B., Williams, R., and Wilkie, F. Prospective study of physical and psychologic factors in elderly men who subsequently suffered acute myocardial infarction. *Clinical Research,* 1973, *21,* 465.

Nowlis, V. The description and analysis of mood. *Annals of the New York Academy of Science,* 1956, *65,* 345–355.

Obrist, W. D. Cerebral physiology of the aged: Relation to psychological function. In N. Burch and H. L. Altshuler (Eds.), *Behavior and Brain Electrical Activity.* New York: Plenum Press, 1975, 421–430.

Obrist, W. D. Problems of aging. In A. Redmond (Ed.), *Handbook of Electroencephalography and Clinical Neurophysiology.* Amsterdam: Elsevier Publishing Co., 1976, 275–292.

Obrist, W. D. Cerebral blood flow and EEG changes associated with aging and dementia. In E. W. Busse and D. G. Blazer (Eds.), *Handbook of Geriatric Psychiatry.* New York: Van Nostrand Reinhold Co., 1980, 83–101.

Obrist, W. D., and Busse, E. W. The electroencephalogram in old age. In W. P. Wilson (Ed.), *Applications of Electroencephalography in Psychiatry.* Durham, N.C.: Duke University Press, 1965, 185–205.

Obrist, W. D., and Busse, E. W. Laboratory Summary, unpublished, 1972.

Obrist, W. D., Busse, E. W., and Henry, C. E. Relation of electroencephalograms to blood pressure in elderly persons. *Neurology,* 1961, *2,* 151–158.

Obrist, W. D., Sokoloff, L., Lassen, N. A., Lane, M. H., Butler, R. N., and Feinberg, I. Relationship of EEG to cerebral blood flow and metabolism in old age. *EEG and Clinical Neurophysiology,* 1963, *15,* 610–619.

Obrist, W. D., Silver, D., Wilkinson, W. E., Harel, D., Heyman, A., and Wang, H. S. The xenon-133 inhalation method: Assessment of rCBF in carotid endarterectomy. Proceedings of the Sixth International Symposium on Cerebral Blood Flow and Metabolism, Philadelphia, 1973.

Obrist, W. D., Thompson, H. K., King, C. H., and Wang, H. S. Determination of regional cerebral blood flow by inhalation of 133-Xenon. *Circulatory Research,* 1967, *20,* 124–135.

Obrist, W. D., Thompson, H. K., Wang, H. S., and Cronquist, S. A simplified procedure for determining fast compartment rCBFs by [133]xenon inhalation. In R. W. R. Russell (Ed.), *Brain and Blood Flow.* Pitman Publishing Co., London, 1971, 11–15.

Palmore, E. The effects of aging on activities and attitudes. *Gerontologist,* 1968, *8,* 259–263.

Palmore, E. (Ed.). *Normal Aging*. Durham, N.C.: Duke University Press, 1970.

Palmore, E. The relative importance of social factors in predicting longevity. In E. Palmore and F. Jeffers (Eds.), *Prediction of Life Span*. Lexington, Mass., 1971.

Palmore, E., and Luikart, C. Health and social factors in life satisfaction. *Journal of Health and Social Behavior*, 1972, *13*, 236–242.

Palmore, E. (Ed.), *Normal Aging II*. Durham, N.C.: Duke University Press, 1974a.

Palmore, E. Predicting longevity: A new method. In E. Palmore (Ed.), *Normal Aging II*. Durham, N.C.: Duke University Press, 1974b, 281–290.

Palmore, E. Facts on aging: A short quiz. *Gerontologist*, 1977, *17*(4), 315–320.

Palmore, E. When can age, period, and cohort be separated? *Social Forces*, 1978a, *57*:1, 282–295.

Palmore, E. Are the aged a minority group. *Journal of the American Geriatric Society*, 1978b, *26*(5), 214–217.

Palmore, E. *Social Patterns in Normal Aging*. Durham, N.C.: Duke University Press, 1981.

Palmore, E., Cleveland, W., Nowlin, J., Ramm, D., and Siegler, I. C. Stress and adaptation in later life. *Journal of Gerontology*, 1979, *34*, 841–851.

Palmore, E., and Jeffers, F. *Prediction of Life Span*. Lexington, Mass.: D. C. Heath, 1971.

Palmore, E. P., Nowlin, J. B., Busse, E. W., Siegler, I. C., and Maddox, G. L. (Eds.), *Normal Aging III*. Durham, N.C.: Duke University Press, 1985.

Pfeiffer, E. Sexual behavior in old age. In E. W. Busse and E. Pfeiffer (Eds.), *Behavior and Adaptation in Later Life*. Boston, Mass.: Little, Brown & Co., 1969, 151–162.

Pfeiffer, E. Survival in old age. In E. Palmore (Ed.), *Normal Aging II*. Durham, N.C.: Duke University Press, 1974, 269–280.

Pfeiffer, E., Verwoerdt, A., and Davis, F. Determinants of sexual behavior in middle and old age. *Journal of American Geriatric Society*, 1972, *20*, 151–158.

Pfeiffer, E., Verwoerdt, A., and Wang, H. S. Sexual behavior in aged men and women. I. Observations on 254 community volunteers. *Archives of General Psychiatry*, 1968, *19*, 753–758.

Poon, L. W., Thompson, L. W., and Marsh, G. R. Average evoked potential changes as a function of processing complexity. *Psychophysiology*, 1976, *13*, 43–49.

Posner, M. I. *Chronometric Exploration of Mind*. Hillsdale, N. J.: Lawrence Erlbaum, 1978.

Posner, M. I., and Snyder, C. R. R. Attention and cognitive control. In R. L. Solso (Ed.), *Information Processing and Cognition: The Loyola Symposium*. Hillsdale, N.J.: Lawrence Erlbaum, 1975.

Post, F. *The Significance of Affective Symptoms in Old Age*. Maudsley Monograph. London: Oxford University Press, 1962, 10.

Prinz, P. N. Sleep patterns in health aged: Relationship with intellectual function. *Journal of Gerontology*, 1977, *32*(2), 192–195.

Pritchard, W. S. Psychophysiology of P300. *Psychological Bulletin*, 1981, *89*, 506–540.

Rabbitt, P. M. A. Set and age in a choice-response task. *Journal of Gerontology*, 1964, *19*, 301–306.

Rabbitt, P. M. A. An age decrement in the ability to ignore irrelevant information. *Journal of Gerontology*, 1965, *20*, 233–238.

Ramm, D. Data screening programs. Technical Report, Duke Center Social Survey Laboratory and Archive, 1980.

Ramm, D., and Cleveland, W. P. A model for error detection in medium sized data bases. Technical Report, Duke Center Social Survey Laboratory and Archive, 1980a.

Ramm, D., and Cleveland, W. P. Error detection in longitudinal studies of aging. Technical Report, Duke Center Social Survey Laboratory and Archive, 1980b.

Ramm, D., and Gianturco, D. T. Data Processing in Longitudinal Studies. In E. Palmore (Ed.), *Normal Aging II*. Durham, N.C.: Duke University Press, 1974, 297–307.

Rao, N. S., Ali, Z. A., Omar, H. M., and Halsey, J. S. Regional cerebral blood flow in acute stroke: Preliminary experience with the [133]xenon inhalation method. Paper presented at the Cerebrovascular Clinical Research Center Workship, Phoenix, 1973.

Riley, M., Johnson, M., and Foner, A. *Aging and Society*, Volume 3. New York: Russell Sage Foundation, 1972.

Rorschach, H. *Psychodiagnostics*. New York: Grune and Stratton, 1942.

Rusin, M., and Siegler, I. C. Personality differences between participants and drop-outs in a longitudinal study. Presentation at annual meetings of Gerontological Society, Louisville, Kentucky, 1975.

SAS Institute, *SAS User's Guide*, 1979 edition, 1979.

Schaie, K. W. A general model for the study of developmental problems.

Psychological Bulletin, 1965, *64*, 92–107.

Schear, J. M., and Nebes, R. D. Memory for verbal and spatial information as a function of age. *Experimental Aging Research*, 1980, *6*, 271–281.

Schenkenberg, T. Visual, auditory, and somatosensory evoked responses of normal subjects from childhood to senescence. Unpublished doctoral dissertation, University of Utah, 1970.

Seymour, P. H. K. Pictorial coding of verbal descriptions. *Quarterly Journal of Experimental Psychology*, 1974, *26*, 39–51.

Siegler, I. C. The terminal drop hypothesis: Fact or artifact? *Experimental Aging Research*, 1975, *1*, 169–185.

Siegler, I. C., Murray, P., Johnson, J., and Rusin, M. *Psychology Technician's Handbook*, Longitudinal Laboratory, Duke University, 1976.

Siegler, I. C. Longitudinal reaction time patterns. Unpublished manuscript, Duke University, 1977.

Siegler, I. C. The psychology of adult development and aging. In E. W. Busse and D. G. Blazer (Eds.), *Handbook of Geriatric Psychiatry*. New York: Van Nostrand Reinhold Co., 1980, 169–221.

Siegler, I. C., and Botwinick, J. Factorial nature of the WAIS. Unpublished manuscript, Duke University, 1980.

Siegler, I. C. Intelligence, reaction time, and memory in young-old vs. old-old participants in the first longitudinal study. In K. W. Schaie and G. Rudinger (Chairs), *Consistency and Change in the Cognitive Functioning of the 'young' old and 'old' old*. Symposium presented at the XIIth International Congress of Gerontology, Hamburg, West Germany, July, 1981.

Siegler, I. C. Psychological aspects of the Duke Longitudinal Studies. In K. W. Schaie (Ed.), *Longitudinal Studies of Psychological Development in Adulthood*. New York: Guilford Press, 1983, pp. 136–190.

Siegler, I. C., and Botwinick, J. A long-term longitudinal study of intellectual ability of older adults: The matter of selective attrition. *Journal of Gerontology*, 1979, *34*(2), 242–245.

Siegler, I. C., and Nowlin, J. B. The interaction of health and behavior in the Duke Longitudinal Studies. Symposium presented at meetings of American Psychological Association, New York, August, 1979.

Siegler, I. C., Gatz, M., Tyler, F., and George, L. K. Aging Competency, Final Report, Administration on Aging, April, 1979.

Siegler, I. C., McCarty, S. M., and Logue, P. E. Wechsler memory scale scores, selective attrition and distance from death. *Journal of Gerontology*, 1982, *37*(2), 176–181.

Siegler, I. C., George, L. K., and Okun, M. Cross-sequential analysis of adult personality. *Developmental Psychology*, 1979, *15*, 350–351.

Smith, J. C., Marsh, J. T., Greenberg, S., and Brown, W. S. Human auditory frequency-following responses to a missing fundamental. *Science*, 1978, *201*, 639–641.

Stokes, R., and Maddox, G. L. Some factors in retirement adaptation. *Journal of Gerontology*, 1967, 22(3), 329–333.

Stroop, J. R. Studies of interference in serial verbal reactions. *Journal of Experimental Psychology*, 1935, *18*, 643–662.

Thompson, L. W., and Wilson, S. Electrocortical reactivity and learning in the elderly. *Journal of Gerontology*, 1966, *21*, 45–51.

Thompson, L. W., Eisdorfer, C., and Estes, E. H. Cardiovascular disease and behavioral changes in the elderly. *Proceedings of the Seventh International Congress of Gerontology*, 1966, 387–390. Reprinted in E. Palmore (Ed.), *Normal Aging*. Durham, N.C.: Duke University Press, 1970, 227–231.

Thompson, L. W., Opton, E., and Cohen, L. D. Effects of age, presentation speed, and sensory modality on performance of a "vigilance" task. *Journal of Gerontology*, 1963, *18*, 366–369.

Tindall, J., and Palmore, E. Skin conditions and lesions in the aged: A longitudinal study. In Palmore, E. (Ed.), *Normal Aging II*, 1974, pp. 18–23.

Tindall, J. P., and Smith, J. G. Skin lesions of the aged. In E. Palmore (Ed.), *Normal Aging*. Durham, N.C.: Duke University Press, 1970, 50–57.

Treisman, A. M. Strategies and models of selective attention. *Psychological Review*, 1969, *76*, 282–299.

Verwoerdt, A., Pfeiffer, E., and Wang, H. S. Sexual behavior in senescence. *Journal of Geriatric Psychiatry*, 1969, *2*, 163–180.

Wang, H. S., and Busse, E. W. EEG of healthy old persons—A longitudinal study. I: dominant background activity and occipital rhythm. *Journal of Gerontology*, 1969, *24*, 419–426.

Wang, H. S., and Busse, E. W. Dementia in old age. In C. Wells (Ed.), *Dementia, Contemporary Neurology Series*. Philadelphia, Pa.: F. A. Davis Co., 1971, 151–162.

Wang, H. S., and Busse, E. W. Heart disease and brain impairment among aged persons. In E. Palmore (Ed.), *Normal Aging II*. Durham, N.C.: Duke University Press, 1974a, 160–167.

Wang, H. S., and Busse, E. W. Brain impairment and longevity. In E. Palmore (Ed.), *Normal Aging II*. Durham, N.C.: Duke University Press, 1974b, 263–268.

Wang, H. S., and Busse, E. W. Correlates of regional blood flow in the elderly community resident. In A. M. Harper, W. B. Jennett, J. D. Miller, and

J. O. Rowan (Eds.), *Blood Flow and Metabolism in the Brain*. London: Churchill Livingstone, 1975, 8.17–1.18.

Wang, H. S., Obrist, W. D., and Busse, E. W. Neurophysiological correlates of the intellectual function of elderly persons living in the community. *American Journal of Psychiatry*, 1970, *126*, 39–46.

Warren, L. R., and Marsh, G. R. Hemispheric asymmetry in the processing of Stroop stimuli. *Bulletin of the Psychonomic Society*, 1978, *12*, 214–216.

Warren, L. R., and Marsh, G. R. Changes in event-related potentials during the processing of Stroop stimuli. *International Journal of Neuroscience*, 1979, *9*, 217–223.

Warren, L. R., Wagener, J. W., and Herman, G. E. Binaural analysis in the aging auditory system. *Journal of Gerontology*, 1978, *33*, 731–736.

Watson, W. E. Memory search, response competition, and aging: The processing of irrelevant information. Unpublished doctoral dissertation, Syracuse University, 1977.

Wechsler, D. A standardized memory scale for clinical use. *Journal of Psychology*, 1945, *19*, 87–95.

Wechsler, D. *Wechsler Adult Intelligence Scale Manual*. New York: Psychological Corporation, 1955.

Whanger, A. D., and Wang, H. S. Vitamin B-12 deficiency in an aging psychiatric population. *Gerontologist*, 1970, *10*, 31–36. Reprinted in E. Palmore (Ed.), *Normal Aging II*. Durham, N.C.: Duke University Press, 1974, 63–73.

Wilkie, F., and Eisdorfer, C. Intelligence and blood pressure in the aged. *Science*, 1971, *172*, 959–962.

Wilkie, F., and Eisdorfer, C. Terminal changes in intelligence. In E. Palmore (Ed.), *Normal Aging II*. Durham, N.C.: Duke University Press, 1974, 103–115.

Wilkie, F., Eisdorfer, C., and Siegler, I. C. Reaction time changes in the aged. 10th International Congress of Gerontology, Jerusalem, Israel, June, 1975. Abstracted in *Proceedings of 10th International Congress of Gerontology*, Vol. 2, 177.

Wilkie, F., Eisdorfer, C., and Nowlin, J. B. Memory and blood pressure in the aged. *Experimental Aging Research*, 1976, *2*, 3–16.

Wilson, R. W. Assessing the Impact of Life Changes and Events. Doctoral dissertation. Durham, N.C.: Duke University, 1980.

Woodbury, M. A. Statistical Record Matching for Files. *Incomplete Data in Survey Samples*. Vol. 3, Session IV. Academic Press, 1983, 173–181.

Woodbury, M. A. Going beyond descriptive uses of correlative methods:

An examination of structural change with age. Presented at the Gerontological Society Meeting, Louisville, Kentucky, October, 1975.

Woodbury, M. A., and Dowdy, L. W. Maximum likelihood estimation for multivariate normal distributions with missing data components. Presented at American Statistical Association, Boston, Mass., 1976.

Woodbury, M., and Manton, K. A new procedure for analysis of medical classification. *Meth. Inform. Med.*, 1982, *21*, 210–220.

Woodbury, M. A., and Orchard, T. A missing information principle: Theory and application. *Proceedings of the Sixty Berkeley Symposium on Mathematical Statistics and Probability* (held at the Statistical Laboratory, University of California, June–July, 1970), University of California Press, 1971, 697–715.

Woodbury, M. A., Manton, K. G., and Siegler, I. C. Evaluation of structural change due to aging, selection and conditioning in the Duke Longitudinal Studies: Markovian analysis of covariance structure. Presented at the Gerontological Society Meeting, Louisville, Kentucky, October, 1975. Technical Report of the Duke Center for the Study of Aging and Human Development.

Woodbury, M., Manton, K., Siegler, I. Markov network analysis: Suggestions for innovations in covariance structure analysis. *Experimental Aging Research*, 1982, *8*, 135–140.

Index

Index

user's guide to data sets, code-
books, and technical reports,
37–39
variables and indices, 24–26
Self-concept, studies of, 90–92
Senile dementia, Alzheimer's type
(SDAT), 69, 76
Serum cholesterol levels, 57
Sexuality and aging, 61–62, 125,
131
Seymour, P. H. K., 98
Shy, M. G., 3
Siegler, I. C., xiii, 23, 24, 27, 58,
78, 79, 80, 81–82, 83, 84, 86, 92
Silverman, A. J., 3
16 Personality Factors (16PF)
Questionnaire, 78, 85, 86
Skin changes, 59
Slow wave activity, 45
Smith, J. C., 114
Smoking, 57
Social factors in experience of
aging, 119–132
age stratification, 126–129
APC problem, 122. *See also* Age/
period/cohort (APC) analysis
conclusions on, 132
disengagement theory, 119,
120–121, 124–126
findings, 124–132
homogeneity and heterogeneity
in aging, 131–132
life events and stress, 129–130.
See also Life events; Stress
problem, statement of, 120–123
research design, 123
role transitions and life events,
122–123
social allocation of resources,
122
social integration and involve-

ment, 124–126
society as a succession of
cohorts, 121
Social gerontology, 119–120
Speech understanding, auditory
changes and, 115–116
Spengler, J., 134
SPSS, 36, 37
Statistical consultation, use of,
36–37
Stereotypes of aging, 129
Sternberg, S., 107, 109
Stokes, R., 131
Stress
CPT, 87–89. *See also* Continuous
performance task
and life events, 89–90, 129–130
perception of, and response
strategies, 92–93
Stroop, J. R., 110

Tape Storage and Retrieval
(TSAR), 10, 35–36
Technical reports, 37–39
Temporal lobe abnormalities, 47
Thaler, M. B., 3
Theoretical perspective on aging,
4–8, 125–139
disengagement theory, 119,
120–121, 124
Theta activity, 45
Thompson, L. W., 49, 80, 87
Tindall, J. P., 59
Treisman, A. M., 110
TSAR, 10, 35–36

VALID, 35
Variables, 24–26
Vascular reactivity in senescence,
62–65
findings, 64–65